MW00716298

ideas

ideas

+interiors
+interiores
+intérieurs
+innenbereich

AUTHORS
Fernando de Haro & Omar Fuentes

EDITORIAL DESIGN & PRODUCTION

AM
EDITORES

PROJECT MANAGERS
Valeria Degregorio Vega
Tzacil Cervantes Ortega

COORDINATION
Susana Madrigal Gutiérrez

COPYWRITER
Roxana Villalobos

ENGLISH TRANSLATION
Louis Loizides

FRENCH TRANSLATION
Architextos: Translation Services and Language Solutions

GERMAN TRANSLATION
Heike Ruttkowski

Ideas
+interiors · +interiores · +intérieurs · +innenbereich

© 2010, Fernando de Haro & Omar Fuentes

AM Editores S.A. de C.V.
Paseo de Tamarindos 400 B, suite 102, Col. Bosques de las Lomas,
C.P. 05120, México, D.F. Tels. 52(55) 5258 0279, Fax. 52(55) 5258 0556.
E-mail: ame@ameditores.com   www.ameditores.com

ISBN 13: 978-607-437-011-9

All rights reserved. No part of this book may be reproduced or copied in any form or by any graphic, electronic or mechanical means, including scanning, photocopying,
photographing, taping, or information storage and retrieval systems -known or unknown-, without the explicit written permission of the publisher(s).
Ninguna parte de este libro puede ser reproducida, archivada o transmitida en forma alguna o mediante algún sistema, ya sea electrónico, mecánico o de
fotorreproducción sin la previa autorización de los editores.
Tous droits réservés. Reproduction, copie et diffusion intégrale ou partielle interdites sous toutes formes et par tous moyens sans le consentement de l'éditeur.
Keine teilen von diesem Buch, kann in irgendeiner Form oder mittels irgendeines Systems reproduziert, übersandt oder abheftet werden, weder elektronisch, mechanisch,
oder fotokopierte ohne die vorausgehende Genehmigung der Redakteure.

Printed in China.

INDEX • INDICE

introduction   introducción

This edition of Ideas Interiors features simple and practical tips on how to create a great atmosphere for different rooms such as lounges, studies, bars, dining rooms and TV rooms, as well as bathrooms, kitchens and bedrooms. The book is packed with ideas on the best way to decorate a home depending on the personality and preferences of the occupants. Its aim is to allow readers to take what they need and best suits their tastes to make their home a place of true satisfaction, which is why it explores everything from the most modern, innovative and exotic trends to more classical styles.

En esta ocasión Ideas Interiores contiene consejos prácticos y sencillos de implementar para conseguir ambientes atractivos en estancias (salas, estudios, bares, comedores, salas de TV), baños, cocinas y recámaras. A lo largo del volumen se plasman suficientes ideas para decorar un hogar de la manera más adecuada y de acuerdo con la forma de pensar y sentir de cada quien. Se trata de que cada uno tome lo que más le convenga y se acople a sus necesidades para que consiga una casa que sea compatible con sus propios gustos. Por ello, se incluyen ideas que abarcan desde lo más moderno, innovador y exótico hasta las tendencias más clásicas.

introduction   einleitung

Cette nouvelle publication de « Ideas Intérieurs » met l'accent sur les conseils pratiques et faciles à suivre pour créer des atmosphères particulières en ce qui concerne les pièces propices à la détente (salons, bureaux, coins bar, salles à manger, salons télé), les salles de bain, les cuisines et les chambres à coucher. Cet ouvrage regorge d'idées en tout genre pour décorer son domicile de la manière la plus adéquate tout en respectant les goûts de chacun. Car le but de ce volume, c'est que tout le monde puisse y trouver ce qu'il recherche, ce qu'il souhaite pour faire de son domicile le cadre idéal pour exprimer ses préférences en matière de décoration.

In dieser Ausgabe enthält "Ideas Innenbereich" praktische und einfach umsetzbare Tipps, um attraktive Atmosphären in Wohnräumen (Wohnzimmer, Studio, Bar, Esszimmer und Fernsehraum), Badezimmer, Küche und Schlafzimmer zu schaffen. Im Verlauf des Buches werden ausreichend Ideen für die Dekoration des Hauses gegeben, die angemessen sind und mit dem Denken und Fühlen eines jeden Bewohners übereinstimmen. Davon kann jeder das auswählen, was seinen Bedüfnissen und Erfordernissen entspricht, damit das Haus so eingerichtet wird, wie es dem jeweiligen Geschmack entspricht. Daher sind Ideen

Some suggestions encourage readers to try out new things, to be daring, to stand at the cutting edge and create new and unexpected effects in their residence, but without overlooking the need for compatible styles. Planning and coordination are essential in decoration.

To help readers achieve this, some basic rules are given on style and harmony and bearing in mind things like color, shape, furnishings, light, space size, fittings and all the objects that play an important role in interior design. The suggestions provided focus on both decorative and functional aspects.

The specific points covered in this volume correspond to the pictures displayed so that readers can see what the possible results look like. These photos show the outcome of the efforts and creativity of renowned architects and interior designers who willingly share the secrets of their respective trades.

Algunas sugerencias animarán al lector a experimentar y a atreverse, a estar a la vanguardia y a crear en los distintos espacios efectos nuevos e inesperados, sin que por ello se concluya en una incoherencia de estilos, pues tampoco se trata de crear una muestra decorativa a voluntad.

Para que esto no ocurra, se relatan algunos principios básicos de armonía y estilo, considerando colores, formas, mobiliario, luz, dimensiones espaciales, accesorios y todos aquellos objetos importantes en el diseño de interiores, buscando que no solamente impliquen sugerencias decorativas sino también funcionales.

Una serie de textos puntuales, que son congruentes con las imágenes que se presentan, permiten visualizar los resultados a los que se puede llegar. Estas fotografías se derivan del trabajo y la creatividad

Aussi les idées présentées ici vont-elles du plus classique au plus moderne, novateur, inhabituel.

Certaines suggestions inciteront le lecteur à l'aventure, aux nouvelles expériences pour se situer à l'avant-garde de la décoration et pour créer différents espaces avec des résultats originaux, modernes et imprévus sans pour autant briser la cohérence des genres utilisés. Car cet ouvrage n'est évidemment pas une présentation de styles sans rapport les uns avec les autres …

Afin d'éviter toutes discordances entre différents genres, ce volume rappelle certains principes de base quant à l'harmonie et aux styles des couleurs, des formes, du mobilier, de la lumière, des dimensions de l'espace, des accessoires et de tous les objets qui jouent un rôle important dans la décoration intérieure. Les suggestions ne sont donc pas simplement décoratives mais aussi fonctionnelles.

von supermodern, innovativ und exotisch bis hin zu klassisch enthalten.

Einige Empfehlungen ermuntern den Leser mutig zu sein und neue Lösungen auszuprobieren, so dass in den verschiedenen Räumen neue und unerwartete Effekte erzielt werden, ohne dass dies den Stil durchbricht, denn es geht nicht darum, die Dekoration willkürlich zu gestalten.

Um dies zu verhindern, werden einige grundlegende Prinzipien in Bezug auf Harmonie und Stil aufgezeigt, wobei Farben, Formen, Möbel, Licht, räumliche Dimensionen, Accesoires und all die wichtigen Gegenstände in Betracht gezogen werden, die das Innendesign ausmachen. Es werden nicht nur dekorative, sondern auch praktische Empfehlungen gegeben.

Die kurzen Texte, die die Bilder beschreiben, machen die Ergebnisse verständlicher, die erzielt werden

The designs offered boast great visual appeal and embody the unbridled freedom to use and compose solutions in accordance with the space in question. The result is a series of exotic, creative and evocative realms governed by the imagination and where rich experiences abound.

The aim of all the different ideas and tips for interior decoration is to allow readers to create their dream home. This is why the volume examines in detail the arrangement, properties and qualities of the different architectural components such as furniture and decorations, providing examples of each case from the overall look to the finishing touch to make the decoration just right.

The book also outlines the importance of space distribution, meticulous selection of materials and the requirements of finishes as vital ingredients in the decoration, along with the quest for balance between look and practicality as the ultimate goal.

de destacados profesionales de la arquitectura y el diseño de interiores, quienes sin recelo comparten sus conclusiones.

Son diseños con mucha personalidad estética, pero que a la vez brindan una profunda libertad de uso y de composición según el espacio al que se adapten, llevando a universos exóticos, creativos y sugerentes dominados por las ideas, así como a conformar experiencias en el espacio interior.

Todas las ideas y consejos de interiorismo van destinados a que cada quien logre la casa de sus sueños y disfrute de ella, por ello se analiza la disposición y se describe detalladamente lo que ocurre tanto con los elementos arquitectónicos como con el mobiliario y objetos decorativos, ejemplificando en cada caso desde aspectos de conjunto hasta el toque final que toda decoración precisa.

Asimismo, también se explica la importancia en la distribución de los espacios, la minuciosa elección de los materiales, junto con la exigencia en los acabados como una base esencial de la decoración, y la búsqueda del equilibrio entre estética y funcionalidad, como su finalidad.

Toute une série de textes accompagnant les photographies du livre expliquent les solutions décoratives que l'on peut obtenir. Ces images illustrent à merveille le travail et la créativité de spécialistes reconnus dans les domaines de l'architecture et de la décoration intérieures. Professionnels du métier, ils n'hésitent pas à partager ainsi leurs secrets avec les lecteurs.

Les designs présentés sont très personnalisés d'un point de vue esthétique mais apportent également une grande liberté au niveau de leur utilisation et de leur composition pour que l'on puisse les adopter dans des espaces différents. Des compositions exotiques, créatives et attrayantes, où les idées priment, voient ainsi le jour et les pièces intérieures se transforment en espaces propices à diverses expériences.

Comme toutes les idées et tous les conseils de cet ouvrage offrent la possibilité à chacun de créer la demeure de ses rêves pour en profiter pleinement, la disposition des éléments utilisés, du mobilier et des objets décoratifs ainsi que leur interaction sont soigneusement décrites. Les exemples sont donc multiples, soulignant aussi bien l'ensemble d'un décor comme l'importance de la touche finale dans un espace donné.

Enfin cet ouvrage n'oublie pas de mentionner le rôle essentiel de la distribution des espaces et il aborde également le thème du choix très méticuleux des matériaux (qui, avec les finitions soignées, constituent la base de toute décoration) et celui de la recherche nécessaire entre équilibre et fonctionnalité, véritable but de tout projet décoratif.

können. Die Fotos zeigen die Arbeit und Kreativität von führenden Architekten und Innendekorateuren, die ohne Vorbehalt ihre Lösungen darbieten.

Es handelt sich um Designs mit viel ästhetischer Persönlichkeit, die gleichzeitig auch eine tiefgreifende Freiheit in Bezug auf Gebrauch und Komposition in Übereinstimmung mit dem jeweiligen Raum bieten, wobei exotische, kreative und anregende Welten aufgezeigt werden, die durch die Ideen bestimmt sind und spezielle Erfahrungen im Innenbereich ermöglichen.

Alle Ideen und Empfehlungen in Bezug auf den Innenbereich sind darauf ausgerichtet, dass jeder Einzelne das Haus seiner Träume schafft und geniessen kann. Aus diesem Grund wird die Aufteilung analysiert und detailliert beschrieben, und dies sowohl in Bezug auf die architektonischen Elemente, wie auch die Möbel und dekorativen Gegenstände. Für jeden Fall werden Beispiele genannt, sowohl im Hinblick auf die Gesamtheit als auch den speziellen Touch jeder einzelnen Dekoration.

Gleichermassen wird die Wichtigkeit der Aufteilung der Bereiche erklärt, die Wahl der Materialien, zusammen mit dem Finish der Oberflächen als wesentliche Grundlage der Dekoration. Dabei wird als Endziel stets ein Gleichgewicht zwischen Ästhetik und Funktionalität gesucht.

rooms
estancias
salles de séjour
wohnzimmer

living rooms
salas
salons
wohnzimmer

THE PUBLIC AREAS OF A HOME require special care because they are intended for the occupants to enjoy and for receiving guests and socializing. The furniture in them should be functional and look right. A good design for the lighting is essential for the decoration. Lounges will always look better if sources of lighting are correctly distributed around them and a good balance is struck between direct and indirect light.

LAS ZONAS PÚBLICAS DE UNA CASA merecen especial atención, pues son sitios igual para el disfrute de los habitantes que para recibir invitados y generar convivencia. Se recomienda que sus muebles sean funcionales y que respondan a una estética. El diseño de iluminación es básico en su decoración. Las estancias se ven favorecidas si se distribuyan diversos puntos de luz y se logra un equilibrio entre la iluminación directa y la indirecta.

LA DECORATION DES PIECES COMMUNES D'UNE MAISON se doit d'être soignée car les occupants aiment y passer du temps et recevoir des invités. Une atmosphère conviviale y est ainsi de rigueur. On recommandera donc un mobilier à la fois fonctionnel et esthétique. Quant à l'éclairage que l'on choisit, c'est en fait la base de la décoration car les salons sont principalement mis en valeur par plusieurs sources de lumière et un certain équilibre entre les éclairages direct et indirect.

DIE ÖFFENTLICHEN BEREICHE EINES HAUSES verdienen besondere Aufmerksamkeit, denn sie werden von den Bewohnern genossen und dienen ferner zum Empfang von Gästen, sowie zum Zusammensein. Die Möbel sollten funktionell sein und einer Ästhetik entsprechen. Das Beleuchtungsdesign ist grundlegend für die Dekoration. Wohnzimmer sehen besonders schön aus, wenn das Licht auf verschiedene Punkte verteilt wird und ein Gleichgewicht zwischen direktem und indirektem Licht erreicht wird.

The depth and length of the space can be brought out to the full by harnessing the tones, patterns and textures of floor and wall coverings and finishes.

Es factible realzar las características de profundidad y longitud del espacio jugando con la tonalidad, el dibujo y la textura de los recubrimientos y acabados de pisos y muros.

Il est possible de mettre en valeur les particularités d'une pièce, sa profondeur et sa longueur, en jouant sur les teintes, les motifs et la texture des revêtements et des finitions du sol et des murs.

Die Tiefe und Länge des Raumes können hervorgehoben werden, indem Farbtöne, Muster und Oberflächen von Böden und Mauern variiert werden.

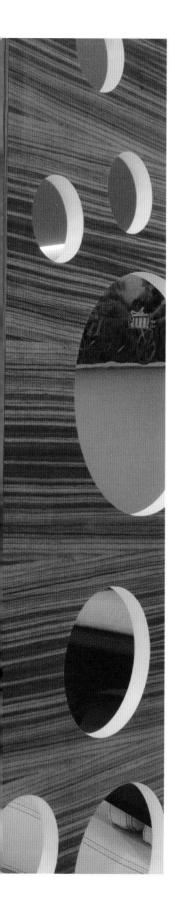

If there is one place in the home where the tastes and
preferences of the occupants find expression, it's the lounge.
The presence of sculptures reveals a fondness for the arts. But
it is essential for these items to be in proportion to the space
and well positioned to prevent them from competing with
each other.

Si algún espacio expresa las preferencias y gustos de sus
habitantes es la sala. La inclusión de figuras escultóricas
habla del interés por el arte. No obstante, es preciso que
estas piezas sean proporcionales al espacio y que sean
colocadas de un modo que no compitan unas con otras.

Si une pièce exprime bien les préférences et les goûts de ses
occupants, c'est sans nul doute le salon. Des sculptures, par
exemple, montrent bien que l'art ne leur est pas indifférent.
Il est néanmoins conseillé que ces œuvres n'occupent
pas une place trop importante dans la pièce ou que l'une
d'entre elles suscite plus d'intérêt que les autres.

Das Wohnzimmer ist der Ort, der in erster Linie die Vorlieben
und Geschmäcker der Bewohner widerspiegelt. Der
Einbezug von Skulpturen spricht von Interesse an der Kunst.
Dennoch sollten sie in Bezug auf ihre Proportionen in den
Raum passen. Ferner sollten sie so angebracht werden, dass
nicht ein Stück mit dem anderen konkurriert.

Gold is traditionally associated with opulence and, as a tone, provides warmth. It combines well with light-colored wood and emphasizes the presence of darkly colored furniture. A touch of gold on an architectural component, such as a small wall or soffit, offers creative design options.

Tradicionalmente el dorado se asocia con la riqueza y es un tono que ofrece calidez; va bien con las maderas claras y hace resaltar el mobiliario negro. Un buen toque en dorado para un elemento arquitectónico –un murete o un plafón, por ejemplo– ofrece una posibilidad original de diseño.

On associe en général les dorures avec la richesse et leurs teintes mettent en valeur la qualité des objets auxquels elles sont associées. Les dorures vont bien sur les bois de couleur claire et font ressortir l'esthétique des meubles noirs. Solution décorative originale, c'est un plus pour certains élément architecturaux comme, par exemple, un petit mur ou un faux-plafond.

Traditionell wird Gold mit Reichtum in Verbindung gebracht, wobei es sich um einen Farbton handelt, der Wärme ausstrahlt. Er passt gut zu hellem Holz und hebt schwarze Möbel hervor. Ein goldener Touch an einem architektonischen Element, wie zum Beispiel einer Mauer oder einer abgehängten Decke, führt zu einem originellen Design.

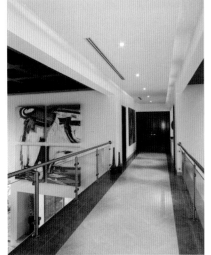

Monochrome settings in lounges are a guarantee of tastefulness and elegance, both of which are easy to achieve by using different beige and brown tones.

Los ambientes monocromáticos en salas hacen sentir sobriedad y elegancia; trabajando con escalas de beiges y cafés es fácil conseguirlos.

Les décorations monochromes pour les salons transforment la pièce en lieu sobre et élégant et elles sont faciles à obtenir en jouant sur les différents tons du beige et du marron.

Monochromatische Atmosphären in Wohnzimmern erwecken den Eindruck von Schlichtheit und Eleganz; wird mit Beige- und Brauntönen gearbeitet, ist dies leicht zu erreichen.

A uniform ambience can be obtained in a living room if the finishes of large areas are made of the same materials and colors. The presence of a more daring object, for instance a "pop art" painting, will draw a boundary between the living room and the dining room.

Cuando en una estancia se procura que los acabados de las grandes superficies coincidan en materiales y colorido se tendrá la sensación de estar frente a una atmósfera unitaria. Será suficiente con introducir algún objeto atrevido para marcar el límite entre sala y comedor; por ejemplo, un cuadro "pop art".

Si l'on utilise les mêmes matériaux pour les finitions d'une salle de séjour qui comprend plusieurs espaces assez vastes, si, qui plus est, ces finitions sont de la même couleur, la sensation d'harmonie que l'on ressentira dans cette pièce sera évidente. On se permettra simplement quelques objets assez audacieux pour séparer le salon de la salle à manger comme, par exemple, un tableau pop'art.

Wenn im Wohnzimmer darauf geachtet wird, dass das Finish von grossen Oberflächen in Bezug auf Farbe und Materialien übereinstimmt, entsteht der Eindruck einer einheitlichen Atmosphäre. Es ist ausreichend, ein gewagtes Objekt zu verwenden, um eine Grenze zwischen Wohn- und Esszimmer zu setzen, wie zum Beispiel ein Bild im Pop Art-Stil.

One way to balance the space is to position furniture with a similar visual impact in a zigzag, leaving the brighter colors at the back to accentuate the sensation of depth.

Una opción para balancear el espacio es ubicar muebles de pesos visuales similares a manera de zig-zag, en tanto que para acentuar la profundidad se deja el color más luminoso al fondo.

Des meubles qui retiennent l'œil, placés en « zigzag » dans la pièce, est un bon moyen d'équilibrer l'espace. Quant aux couleurs les plus vives, elles doivent être situées au fond de la pièce lorsque l'on souhaite en accentuer la profondeur.

Eine Möglichkeit zum Erzielen eines Gleichgewichtes im Raum ist das Aufstellen der Möbel mit gleichem visuellem Gewicht in Zick-Zack-Form, wobei zur Betonung der Tiefe der hellste Farbton im Hintergrund stehen sollte.

A harmonious repetition of elements, such as niches, vases or lamps, including the furniture, sets a rhythm and defines a look.

La repetición armónica de elementos, ya sean nichos, floreros o lámparas, incluyendo el mobiliario, marca un ritmo y precisa una estética.

La répétition de certains éléments architecturaux, que ce soit des niches dans les murs, des vases, des lampes, voire même certains meubles, donne du rythme à l'esthétique choisie et la précise.

Die harmonische Wiederholung von Elementen, gleichgültig ob Nischen, Vasen oder Lampen, die Möbel mit inbegriffen, markiert einen Rhythmus und präzisiert die Ästhetik.

Modern-day decorative trends include combining items of furniture of different styles with different finishes, even though the ideal thing is for one style to be clearly prevalent and then punctuated by the furniture of the less dominant style. Classical furniture is a good option when it has the upper hand over contemporary furniture and vice-versa.

Entre las tendencias decorativas actuales se encuentra el combinar muebles de distintos estilos y con acabados diversos; sin embargo, es deseable que prevalezca notoriamente un estilo y que se irrumpa con algunas piezas de otro. Los muebles clásicos van bien cuando dominan sobre los contemporáneos y viceversa.

Une des dernières tendances de la mode en matière de décoration consiste à utiliser pour un salon des meubles de styles divers avec des finitions variées. Il est cependant conseillé de choisir un style précis pour une pièce que l'on pourra modifier ici et là avec quelques éléments qui n'en font pas partie. Les meubles classiques vont très bien associés à quelques meubles modernes. L'inverse est aussi vrai.

Unter den aktuellen Dekorationstrends befindet sich die Kombination von Möbeln mit unterschiedlichem Stil und Finish. Dennoch ist es empfehlenswert, dass eine Stilrichtung deutlich vorherrscht und durch einige Stücke einer anderen Stilrichtung ergänzt wird. Klassische Möbel sind geeignet, wenn ein moderner Stil vorherrscht und umgekehrt.

If the space is distributed in a creative way, one good option is to decorate it with materials that bring a sense of vitality to the area. Good results are guaranteed if they are used on more spacious surfaces. Wood and concrete have character and can be combined to balance the warmth and coldness in an area. To create divisions in solutions of this type, it is a good idea to use a blind wall or any type of partition that obstructs visibility and interrupts the area's continuity. It is advisable to use transparent materials or architectural components located at a certain distance from each other.

Cuando se cuenta con un área de dimensiones interesantes vale la pena decorar con materiales. Elegir aquéllos cuyas características físicas imprimen fuerza al espacio y utilizarlos en amplias superficies es un recurso de diseño infalible. La madera y el concreto aparente poseen personalidad y combinados equilibran calidez y frialdad. Si se desea crear algunas divisiones en este tipo de soluciones se aconseja evitar muros ciegos o cualquier bloque que obstruya la visibilidad e interrumpa la continuidad, es preferible recurrir a transparencias o a elementos arquitectónicos colocados a distancia unos de otros.

Lorsque les dimensions sont assez importantes, il est intéressant d'utiliser certains matériaux pour la décoration en optant pour ceux qui donneront de la force à l'espace. Le procédé est infaillible si on les place sur de grandes surfaces. Le bois et le béton apparent possèdent leurs propres caractéristiques et, associés l'un à l'autre, ils apportent à la fois chaleur et fraîcheur à l'endroit. Lorsque l'on souhaite créer des séparations, il est recommandé d'éviter les murs aveugles ou tout autre obstacle à la visibilité et à la continuité de la pièce. Il est préférable d'avoir recours à des éléments transparents ou à des éléments architecturaux loin les uns des autres.

Wenn über einen Raum verfügt wird, der interessante Dimensionen aufweist, sollte mit Materialien dekoriert werden. Es sollten diejenigen Materialien verwendet werden, die dem Raum Stärke verleihen. Werden sie an grossen Oberflächen angebracht, so ist dies eine unfehlbare Designlösung. Holz und blossliegender Beton besitzen Persönlichkeit und schaffen ein Gleichgewicht zwischen Wärme und Kälte. Sollen Abgrenzungen zwischen dieser Art von Lösungen geschaffen werden, sollten Blindmauern oder jede Art von Wand vermieden werden, die die Sicht und die Kontinuität stören. Hier sollte lieber auf Transparenzen zurückgegriffen werden, oder auf architektonische Elemente, die in einem gewissen Abstand zueinander angebracht werden.

It does not matter whether the decorative style is classical or ultramodern - or anything else for that matter -, the greatest appeal of a lounge lies in its overall composition and will be defined by the size of the furniture and its arrangement in the room. Lounges made up of modules, as inspired by Italian design, offer an array of imaginative arrangement options and the sheer power of their design will infuse the area with character. Furthermore, the benefit of modular arrangements is that the distribution can be changed constantly to create new, vibrant and flexible settings.

No importa si se trata de una decoración clásica o ultramoderna, cualquiera que sea su estilo, el mayor atractivo de una sala se halla en la composición total y son la masividad del mobiliario y su disposición los que la definen. Las salas conformadas por módulos, inspiradas en el diseño italiano, permiten ingeniosos acomodos y gracias a la fuerza de su diseño le dan carácter a esta área. Además, la modularidad ofrece la ventaja de poder modificar constantemente la distribución, consiguiendo cada vez un ambiente renovado, dinámico y flexible.

Quel que soit le style choisi, du classique au plus ultramoderne, ce qui fait l'esthétique d'une pièce réside dans l'ensemble de l'endroit, soit donc dans le poids et la disposition du mobilier. Les salles de séjour de style italien, c'est-à-dire divisées en plusieurs espaces, permettent d'ingénieux aménagements et la force de ce design particulier donne du caractère aux lieux. De plus, les divers espaces offrent la possibilité de pouvoir toujours modifier la disposition de l'ensemble avec, chaque fois, une atmosphère renouvelée, dynamique et souple.

Gleichgültig ob es sich um eine klassische oder supermoderne Dekoration handelt und auch unabhängig von der Stilrichtung, ist die grösste Attraktion eines Wohnzimmers die gesamte Komposition und die Massivität der Möbel, sowie deren Anordnung. Wohnzimmer mit Modulen im italienischen Design ermöglichen gewitzte Aufstellungen und dank der Stärke ihres Designs, verleihen sie diesem Bereich Charakter. Ferner bieten Module den Vorteil, dass sie ständig neu angeordnet werden können, wobei eine neue, dynamische und flexible Atmosphäre erzielt wird.

Folding screens, partitions and lattices are a useful way of separating spaces within the public area but without actually separating them from each other to allow the unobstructed flow of light and air. At the same time, their visual impact means that care must be taken with their appearance, and they should also be seen as decorative tools, which is why their finishes must be impeccable.

Biombos, mamparas y celosías son útiles en las áreas públicas para separar zonas sin aislarlas, permitiendo el libre paso de la luz y el aire. Sin embargo, por su importancia visual es determinante cuidar su estética y verlos también como recursos decorativos, razón por la que sus acabados deben ser impecables.

Paravents et séparations en lattes de bois ou fabriquées avec d'autres matériaux sont utiles pour diviser l'espace sans pour autant le cloisonner car la lumière et l'air peuvent continuer d'y circuler. Il faut toutefois soigner l'esthétique de ces éléments car ils attirent le regard. Solutions décoratives à part entière, leurs finitions doivent être impeccables.

Wandschirme, Trennwände und Schalousien sind nützlich in öffentlichen Bereichen, um sie abzutrennen, ohne sie zu isolieren, wobei das Licht und die Luft nicht beeinträchtigt werden. Dennoch sollte aufgrund ihrer visuellen Wichtigkeit die Ästhetik nicht vernachlässigt werden. Sie sind als dekorative Ressourcen anzusehen und daher sollten ihre Oberflächen einwandfrei sein.

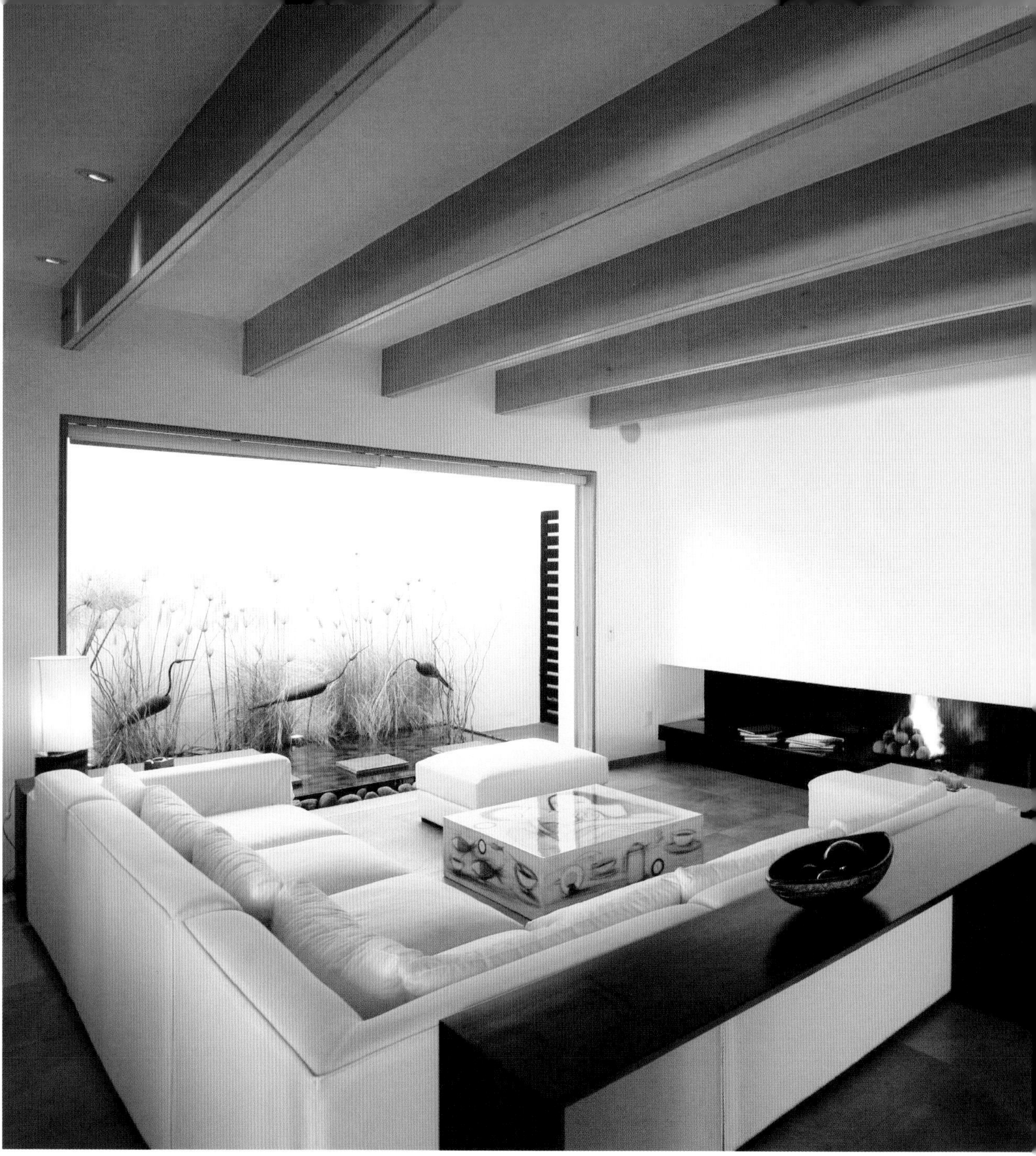

When it comes to choosing the decoration for a double height space, it is vital to bear in mind that some walls are over six meters tall and become spacious backgrounds. The best bet is to leave them blank and spice up the area with sculptures placed in ascending order.

Al definir la decoración de un espacio de doble altura es necesario comprender que algunos muros rebasan los seis metros, por lo que se convierten en telones de fondo. Lo mejor es dejarlos en blanco y complementar la estética con piezas escultóricas colocadas de forma ascendente.

Lorsque l'on définit la décoration d'une pièce en double hauteur, il faut bien comprendre que certains murs dépassent les six mètres de haut. Véritables toiles de fond, le mieux est de les faire peindre en blanc et d'ajouter à la décoration quelques sculptures hautes et élancées.

Bei der Definition der Dekoration eines Raumens mit doppelter Deckenhöhe ist zu berücksichtigen, dass einige Wände mehr als sechs Meter hoch sind. Aus diesem Grund fungieren sie als Hintergrund. Sie sollten am besten weiss gelassen werden und ihre Ästhetik mit Skulpturen ergänzt werden, die aufsteigende Formen aufweisen.

A good way to create an ambience that will impress and define a certain area is to design a wall with a spectacular texture long enough to run the full length of the room.

Para crear una atmósfera impactante y delimitar un área se puede diseñar un muro cuya longitud recorra todo el espacio de la estancia y que posea una textura espectacular.

Si l'on souhaite diviser une pièce avec un élément décoratif audacieux, il est possible d'envisager un mur à la texture spectaculaire dont la longueur recouvrira toute la dimension de la salle de séjour.

Um eine beeindruckende Atmosphäre zu schaffen und einen Bereich abzugrenzen, kann eine Wand aufgestellt werden, deren Länge das gesamte Wohnzimmer durchquert und eine spektakuläre Textur aufweist.

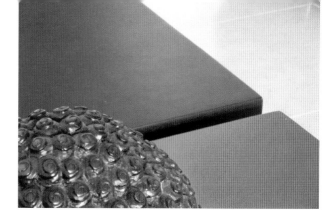

A sizeable, bright red component sharing a space with dark woods and leather upholstery is visually rich enough for a living room.

Un elemento de gran magnitud, en intenso color rojo, compartiendo el área con maderas oscuras y tapicerías de piel es suficiente para vestir la sala de una casa.

Pour habiller la salle de séjour d'une maison, il suffit parfois d'associer une grande surface peinte en rouge vif avec des bois de couleur foncée et des éléments en cuir.

Ein grosses Element in einem intensiven Rotton, das den Bereich mit dunklem Holz und Lederbezügen teilt, ist ausreichend um das Wohnzimmer eines Hauses zu dekorieren.

The textures of materials and the patterns of textiles are ideal for experimentation. Even if the latter option has lost momentum in recent years, cushions and rugs with patterns are still ideal for defining accents and livening up the lounge.

Es tan válido jugar con las texturas de los materiales como con los estampados de los textiles; aún cuando esta última opción ha perdido terreno, los cojines y tapetes con dibujos siguen siendo ideales para conseguir acentos y vivificar la sala.

Deux solutions aussi valables l'une que l'autre : jouer sur les textures des matériaux et sur les motifs des tissus. Même si cette dernière possibilité n'est plus trop utilisée aujourd'hui, les coussins et autres tapis de couleurs variées sont toujours utiles pour faire de la salle de séjour un endroit original et dynamique.

Es können sowohl die Texturen der Materialien als auch die Muster der Textilien variiert werden. Auch wenn die letztere Alternative nicht mehr so häufig Anwendung findet, sind Kissen und Decken mit Mustern weiterhin ideal, um Akzente zu setzen und das Wohnzimmer zu beleben.

bars and cellars
bares y cavas
bars et caves
bars und weinkeller

THE BAR OF A HOUSE NEEDS TO BE both enjoyable and functional, as the pleasure afforded by this space depends not only on a good drink but also on its atmosphere. If the bar is attached to the cellar, the design should be in accordance with the available space. One way to bring out the full splendor of the area is to set the cellar against the perimeter walls and highlight the space by putting a mirror at the back.

LOS BARES DE LAS CASAS deben ser placenteros y funcionales, pues la conquista de este espacio no sólo depende de la buena bebida, sino también de su ambiente. Cuando el bar queda integrado a la cava es importante que el diseño sea acorde con la dimensión espacial. Una alternativa para aprovechar el área es adosar la cava a algunos de los muros perimetrales y realzar el área colocando un espejo al fondo.

LE BAR DANS UNE MAISON doit être un lieu de plaisir fonctionnel car la boisson seule ne suffit pas pour créer une ambiance agréable. Lorsque le bar fait partie de la cave, il est important que le design soit proportionnel aux dimensions de l'endroit. Placer les bouteilles contre certain des murs est une bonne solution pour profiter de l'espace et on peut souligner l'esthétique de la pièce avec un miroir dans le fond.

HAUSBARS sollten praktisch und gemütlich sein, denn dieser Ort sollte nicht nur schmackhafte Getränke bieten, sondern auch eine angenehme Atmosphäre. Befindet sich die Bar im Inneren des Weinkellers ist es wichtig, dass das Design mit der räumlichen Dimension übereinstimmt. Eine Alternative ist die Anbringung des Weinkellers an einer Wand, wobei der Bereich durch einen Spiegel im Hintergrund hervorgehoben werden kann.

Bars need an array of essential utensils such as an ice bucket, bottle opener, corkscrew, cocktail shakers, mixers and different types of glasses, among other things. However, there are no set rules for the furnishings, which will ultimately be defined by taste, preference and specific needs. Wood and leather are a classic double act for the furniture, although a combination of woods can also look great when the different tones are brought out. Another good option for the cellar is furniture that can be concealed by some kind of sliding system.

Un bar tiene que estar equipado con una serie de utensilios esenciales para su operación, como son hielera, destapador, descorchador, cocteleras, mezcladores, vasos y copas, entre otros. Sin embargo, el amueblado no tiene una regla fija sino es cuestión de gustos, preferencias y necesidades particulares. La mancuerna madera y piel es un clásico para el mobiliario; no obstante, la combinación de maderas es también muy lucidora cuando se destacan sus diferencias tonales. Es igualmente útil pensar en muebles de cava que se puedan ocultar a través de un sistema deslizable.

Un bar doit être équipé de manière adéquate pour qu'il soit fonctionnel et doit comprendre, entre autres ustensiles, un sceau à glace, un ouvre-bouteille, un tire-bouchon, des shakers, des verres à mélange, des verres et des coupes. En ce qui concerne le mobilier, il n'existe pas de règles bien précises car c'est une question de goût, de préférences personnelles et de besoin. L'association bois et cuir est très classique pour ce genre d'endroit mais utiliser des bois différents est également très esthétique surtout lorsque l'on peut admirer plusieurs de leurs tons. Il est aussi utile d'opter pour un système coulissant qui permet de dissimuler les meubles de la cave.

Eine Bar muss mit einigen grundlegenden Utensilien ausgerüstet sein, die zu deren Betrieb erforderlich sind, wie zum Beispiel Eiswürfel, Flaschenöffner, Korkenzieher, Cocktailshaker, Mixer, Gläser und Kelche. Dennoch gibt es für die Möblierung keine festen Regeln, sondern es handelt sich vielmehr um eine Frage von Geschmack, Vorlieben und besonderen Erfordernissen. Die Kombination von Holz und Leder ist klassisch für die Möbel. Dennoch ist auch die Kombination von Holz sehr schön, wenn die verschiedenen Farbtöne hervorgehoben werden. Es ist gleichermassen praktisch, wenn die Möbel des Weinkellers durch ein Schiebesystem verborgen werden können.

Highchairs, low chairs and stools are a welcome presence in the bar area. For the first two, the seats and backrests must be comfortable and they must have footrests. A sound system and TV are a great complement for a good chat or for watching a program.

Tanto sillas altas como sillones bajos y taburetes van bien en la zona de bar; en el caso de las primeras es importante que sus asientos y respaldos sean cómodos y tengan apoyos para los pies. Un equipo de sonido y una televisión sirven de complemento para amenizar la plática o disfrutar de un programa.

Les fauteuils bas ou les tabourets conviennent parfaitement à un bar. C'est aussi le cas des chaises hautes mais il est important que leur siège et leur dossier soient confortables et qu'elles comprennent des appuis pour les pieds. Une chaîne stéréo, une télévision peuvent être envisagées pour égayer les conservations ou apprécier une retransmission.

Sowohl Hochstühle als auch niedrige Sessel und Hocker passen gut in den Bereich einer Bar. Im ersten Fall ist es wichtig, dass die Sitze und Rückenlehnen bequem sind und über Stützen für die Füsse verfügen. Eine Stereoanlage und ein Fernseher ergänzen die Harmonie des Gesprächs oder ermöglichen das Geniessen des Programmes.

The bar might sometimes share a space with the dining room or lounge and, while these different sectors need to be harmonized, this does not mean that they can't each have their own identity. A range of contrasting materials in the two areas can create a very pleasant effect and provide each one with personality. An onyx bar top, for instance, will generate a satisfying contrast with the soft textures of the upholstery or the polished wooden surfaces. Another example is the contrast between the warmth of the chimney and the coldness evoked by the mirror.

En algunas ocasiones el bar comparte espacio con el comedor o la sala y, si bien conviene que armonicen, ello no significa que deban tener la misma identidad. Jugar con una paleta de materiales en ambas zonas y contrastarla puede producir un efecto atractivo y dotar de personalidad a cada área. Por ejemplo, una barra de bar de ónix actúa por contraste frente a las suaves texturas de la tapicería o a las superficies pulidas de madera; en otro ejemplo, la chimenea ofrece un aspecto cálido y el espejo evoca frialdad.

Un bar peut parfois être situé dans une salle à manger ou un salon. Même si l'on doit veiller à l'harmonie des lieux, ceci ne veut pas dire qu'ils doivent être identiques. Grâce à toute une gamme de matériaux dans les deux endroits, il est possible de créer un certain contraste assez esthétique et de personnaliser chaque espace. Un comptoir en onyx, par exemple, s'opposera aux délicates textures des tapis et des surfaces polies en bois. Autre exemple : une cheminée réchauffant les lieux associée à un miroir qui apporte de la fraîcheur.

In einigen Fällen befindet sich die Bar im Esszimmer oder Wohnzimmer und –obwohl sie harmonieren sollten- muss die Stilrichtung nicht dieselbe sein. Es können unterschiedliche Paletten an Materialien Verwendung finden, wobei der Kontrast einen attraktiven Effekt hervorrufen kann und jedem Bereich Persönlichkeit verleiht. So kontrastiert zum Beispiel eine Bar aus Onyx mit den weichen Texturen der Bezüge oder den polierten Oberflächen des Holzes. Ein anderes Beispiel ist ein offener Kamin, der einen warmen Aspekt bietet und mit dem Spiegel in Kontrast steht, der Kälte ausstrahlt.

Liqueurs should be kept at room temperature, so it does not really matter if the furniture they are stored in is open or closed. When it comes to wine it is a different story because wine needs to be kept in an isolated place with enough shelves to store the bottles over long periods of time and where factors like humidity, temperature, light, vibrations and ventilation can be controlled. The isolation does not necessarily have to be absolute, and the cellar may visually merge into the rest of the area through glass walls or windows.

Los licores pueden quedar a la intemperie, por lo que no importa si sus muebles de guardado son abiertos o cerrados. Si se trata de vinos las condiciones cambian, pues éstos necesitan ser resguardados en un lugar aislado, donde exista la estantería necesaria para almacenar las botellas durante largos períodos y se tenga el control estricto sobre factores como humedad, temperatura, iluminación, vibración y ventilación. Para que el aislamiento no sea total y la cava pueda compartir visualmente con el resto del área se puede utilizar vidrio en los cerramientos.

Les bouteilles d'alcool pouvant rester à l'air libre, il n'est pas important que les meubles les contenant soient ouverts ou fermés. Ce n'est pas le cas des vins qui ont besoin d'être conservés dans des lieux séparés et de dimensions assez importantes pour y rester longtemps. Qui plus est, l'humidité, la température, l'éclairage, les vibrations et l'aération doivent être rigoureusement contrôlés. Pour que la cave ne soit pas complètement isolée et afin de pouvoir l'admirer, les séparations utilisées peuvent être en verre.

Der Alkohol kann ruhig sichtbar aufbewahrt werden, daher kann das Möbel offen oder geschlossen sein. Wenn es allerdings um Wein geht, sind bestimmte Bedingungen erforderlich, denn Wein muss in einem abgeschlossenen Bereich aufbewahrt werden, auf Weinregalen, wo er über einen langen Zeitraum verbleiben kann und eine strikte Kontrolle über Feuchtigkeit, Temperatur, Beleuchtung, Vibration und Lüftung möglich ist. Damit die Abgrenzung nicht zu krass ist und der Weinkeller visuell in den restlichen Bereich integriert ist, können Glasscheiben mit Verschluss verwendet werden.

One highly attractive possibility is to turn the bar into an architectural element that performs both a decorative and functional role. This could involve designing a series of modular wooden boxes with folding doors, with scattered, low intensity light and low temperature to conserve the drinks. When the doors are opened, the lighting will transform the bar into a sculptural masterpiece. A dynamic and ever-changing item of furniture can be achieved by alternating the opening and closing of the doors.

Resulta muy atractivo convertir un bar en un elemento arquitectónico que también se conciba como decorativo y como mueble funcional. Una opción es diseñar una serie de cajas modulares hechas en madera, con puertas abatibles, a las que se les integre luz dispersa, de poca potencia e intensidad fría con el fin de conservar las bebidas adecuadamente. Cuando las puertas estén abiertas, la iluminación hará lucir el bar como un objeto escultórico. Dado que se podrá jugar alternando la apertura y cierre de puertas, se tendrá un cuerpo dinámico y siempre cambiante.

Faire du bar un élément à part entière de la décoration est très judicieux, en particulier lorsque l'on parvient à en faire un meuble aussi esthétique que fonctionnel. Une solution pour y parvenir consiste à utiliser des caissons en bois, refermés par des portes à abatants et éclairés par une lumière diffuse, peu intense ou froide de façon à conserver les boissons de manière adéquate. Lorsque les portes sont ouvertes, l'éclairage apporte une certaine esthétique au bar pour le transformer en sculpture de grande dimension. Etant donné que l'on peut jouer sur l'alternance entre portes fermées et ouvertes, la décoration du bar se caractérisera par son dynamisme et ses changements continuels.

Es ist sehr attraktiv, wenn eine Bar in ein architektonisches Element verwandelt wird, das auch eine dekorative Funktion übernimmt und gleichzeitig praktisch ist. Eine Möglichkeit ist das Design von modularen Schachteln aus Holz und mit Klapptüren, in die gestreutes Licht integriert wird, das eine geringe Potenz und eine kalte Intensität aufweist, damit die Getränke angemessen aufbewahrt werden. Wenn die Türen geöffnet sind, verwandelt die Beleuchtung die Bar in ein bildhauerisches Objekt. Da die Türen entweder geöffnet oder geschlossen werden können, handelt es sich um einen dynamischen Gegenstand, der Veränderungen zulässt.

TV ROOMS offer an interesting range of possibilities and can assume the guise of movie theaters, libraries or studies. Other options include simpler rooms for enjoying TV, but all of them must be conducive to socializing and relaxation. The decoration must be functional and consistent with the concept, for example, a study will house bookshelves and a desk. It is important to make sure that one activity does not hamper the other.

LA SALAS DE TV pueden obedecer a múltiples conceptos, a veces pueden ser salas de cine, bibliotecas o estudio; otras más simplemente cuartos para disfrutar de la televisión; pero todas deben incitar a la convivencia y al relajamiento. Su decoración tiene que estar en sincronía con el concepto y ser funcional, por ejemplo, un estudio se acompaña de librero y mesa de trabajo, cuidando que el desarrollo de una actividad no obstaculice el de la otra.

LES SALONS TELE peuvent revêtir différentes identités : on peut les aménager comme des petites salles de cinéma, des bibliothèques ou des bureaux. Parfois, ce ne sont que de simples pièces pour regarder la télévision. Mais tous doivent être des lieux conçus pour la vie commune, la détente, et la décoration doit correspondre à leur fonction. Un bureau, par exemple, contient des étagères pour les livres et documents ainsi qu'une table de travail et on doit pouvoir l'utiliser en tout confort.

FERNSEHZIMMER können verschiedene Funktionen gleichzeitig erfüllen, sie können als Kino, Bibliothek oder Studio dienen, oder einfach als Raum zum gemütlichen fernsehen. All diese Funktionen implizieren Zusammensein und Entspannung. Die Dekoration muss mit dem Konzept im Einklang stehen und praktisch sein; so kann zum Beispiel ein Studio durch ein Bücherregal und einen Arbeitstisch ergänzt werden, wobei darauf zu achten ist, dass eine Aktivität die andere nicht stört.

tv rooms
salas de tv
salons télé
fernsehzimmer

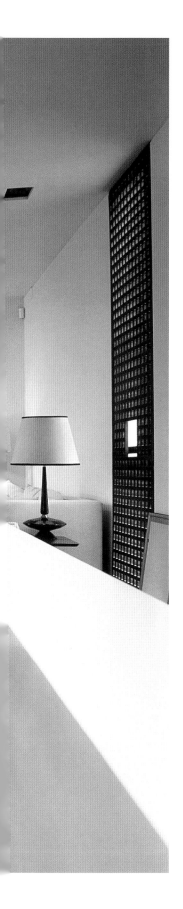

If the TV room is a completely open space, it is a good idea to have a square-shaped item of furniture dividing the living space from the area of movement. A couple of table lamps, one at each end, will provide the ideal complement for such a furniture arrangement.

Cuando una sala de televisión se ubica en un espacio totalmente abierto es aconsejable un mueble en escuadra que delimite el espacio de estar y lo diferencie de la zona de circulación. Un par de lámparas de mesa a los costados complementa bien este tipo de amueblado.

Lorsqu'un salon télé fait partie d'une pièce complètement ouverte, un meuble en forme de L est conseillé pour séparer l'espace détente des lieux de passage. Deux lampes de chevet situées de chaque côté compléteront harmonieusement ce type de mobilier.

Wenn sich das Fernsehzimmer in einem komplett offenen Raum befindet ist es ratsam, ein Möbel im Winkel aufzustellen, das den Wohnbereich abtrennt und ihn vom Durchgangsbereich abgrenzt. Ein paar Tischlampen an den Seiten ergänzen diese Art von Möblierung auf angemessene Weise.

Where the item of furniture that houses the TV goes will depend on the available space. But this furniture should ideally be set against a wall and have compartments that can be used for keeping books or records in or as decorative niches.

De la forma del espacio del que se disponga depende la ubicación del mueble de TV. Sin embargo, éste preferentemente debe de estar adosado a algún muro y contar con compartimentos que puedan ser utilizados para colocar libros o discos, o bien funcionar como nichos decorativos.

L'emplacement du meuble de la télé dépend de la forme de la pièce. Il est toutefois préférable que ce dernier soit placé contre un mur et qu'il comprenne des tiroirs et des étagères ouvertes ou fermées pour y ranger, par exemple, des disques et des livres ou pour y placer des objets décoratifs.

Von der Form des Raumes hängt der Standort des Fernsehmöbels ab. Dennoch sollte es vorzugsweise an eine Wand gelehnt sein und über Fächer verfügen, die zum Unterbringen von Büchern und CDs geeignet sind, beziehungsweise als dekorative Nischen genutzt werden können.

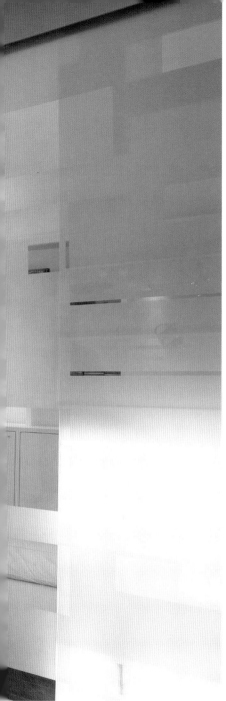

The clarity of a space does not depend exclusively on the presence of daylight or artificial light; it also depends on the colors used on the bigger surfaces and the furniture. The different options available give rise to a whole host of different atmospheres. White, for instance, generates a sensation of cleanliness and accentuates the impression of tidiness; red and brown tones make for a stylish and somewhat uncomplicated ambience, while a combination of dark tones and bright colors creates a more balanced environment.

La claridad de un lugar no solamente se consigue con la luz natural o artificial con la que se cuente, sino también depende del colorido de las grandes superficies y del mobiliario. Desde luego, las atmósferas pueden variar mucho entre una elección y otra. El blanco favorece la sensación de nitidez y exalta la impresión de orden, los tonos rojizos y chocolate ofrecen ámbitos elegantes con tendencia a ser sombríos, en tanto que la mezcla de matices oscuros y colores brillantes genera ambientes más equilibrados.

La clarté d'un endroit n'est pas simplement due à la lumière naturelle ou artificielle à disposition. Les couleurs choisies pour les grandes surfaces murales et le mobilier sont également importantes. L'atmosphère que l'on souhaite créer dépend évidemment du choix que l'on fait. Le blanc donne à la pièce un aspect propre et souligne l'ordre qui y règne alors que les teintes rougeâtres et chocolat en font un lieu élégant mais un peu sombre. Quant aux associations entre couleurs foncées et vives, elles favorisent plus les atmosphères équilibrées.

Die Klarheit eines Ortes hängt nicht nur vom natürlichen oder künstlichen Licht ab, sondern auch von der Farbe der grossen Oberflächen und Möbel. Die Atmosphären bei Wahl der einen oder anderen Alternative können sehr unterschiedlich sein. Die Farbe weiss begünstigt den Eindruck von Schärfe und Ordnung, rötliche und bräunliche Farbtöne führen zu eleganten Atmosphären und tendieren dazu, ein bisschen düster zu wirken. Eine Mischung aus dunklen Tönen und leuchtenden Farben sieht ausgewogener aus.

The range of furniture for housing a TV set available on the market will allow the occupants to decide whether the TV is to be embedded or set on a fixed or multifunctional item of furniture.

La variedad de muebles de TV que existe en el mercado permite definir si se prefiere que la televisión vaya empotrada o que se coloque en un mueble fijo o incluso en un multifuncional.

Le marché propose aujourd'hui un si grand nombre de meubles télé qu'il est possible de disposer d'un téléviseur encastré ou suspendu à un meuble fixe ou multifonction.

Die Vielfalt an Fernsehmöbeln, die auf dem Markt erhältlich sind, ermöglicht die Wahl, ob der Fernseher an der Wand montiert werden soll oder auf einem festen Möbel steht, das sogar multifunktionell sein kann.

Floor to ceiling curtains are back in fashion. The thicker ones offer good protection from the light while watching TV. A great effect can be obtained by contrasting the smoothness of their texture with the roughness of the walls.

Las cortinas de piso a techo vuelven a ponerse de moda. Aquéllas que son gruesas resultan muy útiles para proteger de la luz mientras se ve televisión. Si se contrasta la suavidad de su textura con la rugosidad de los muros se puede obtener un efecto potente

Les rideaux qui vont du sol au plafond sont de nouveau à la mode et les rideaux épais sont très utiles pour regarder la télévision sans être gêné par la lumière. En contrastant la délicatesse de leurs tissus avec l'aspérité des murs, l'effet produit est assez remarquable.

Vorhänge vom Boden bis zur Decke sind wieder modern. Dicke Vorhänge sind geeignet, um vor Licht zu schützen, wenn ferngesehen wird. Kontrastiert die weiche Textur mit der rauhen Wand, so wird ein starker Effekt erzielt.

Two basic qualities of a TV room are comfort and functionality. This is why it is a good idea to understand what the requirements of these areas are and plan solutions in advance. It is also advisable to take into account the placing of curtains or blinds that stop daylight from affecting the sharpness of the TV picture. Furthermore, the seating should be really comfortable and its upholstery pleasant to the touch. The inclusion of one or two small, easy-to-move tables for day-to-day use is another variant that can be considered.

Confort y funcionalidad son dos aspectos fundamentales en un cuarto de televisión. Por ello, se recomienda conocer bien las necesidades de estas zonas y planear sus soluciones oportunamente. Es aconsejable prever la colocación de cortinas o persianas que eviten que la luz natural interfiera con la nitidez de las imágenes que se transmiten en la TV. También se recomienda que los sillones sean muy cómodos y que cuenten con tapicerías agradables al tacto. Incluir una o varias mesitas de uso diario que se muevan con facilidad es otro factor a considerar.

Un salon télé doit être à la fois confortable et fonctionnel. Il est donc recommandé de bien prévoir ce dont on aura besoin dans ces lieux et d'envisager des solutions à l'avance. Il est conseillé, par exemple, de choisir un endroit pour y placer des rideaux ou des stores pour ne pas que la lumière altère la qualité des images retransmises. Les fauteuils doivent également être confortables et il est préférable que leurs tissus soient agréables au toucher. Une ou plusieurs tables basses que l'on utilisera tous les jours et que l'on pourra déplacer à loisir ne seront pas non plus superflues.

Komfort und Funktionalität sind zwei grundlegende Aspekte in einem Fernsehzimmer. Daher sollten die Erfordernisse in diesem Bereich gut analysiert und die Lösungen auf geeignete Weise geplant werden. Es sollten Vorhänge oder Schalousien angebracht werden, die verhindern, dass das natürliche Licht die Bilder stört, die im Fernsehen zu sehen sind. Ferner sollten die Sessel sehr bequem und mit Bezügen versehen sein, die sich angenehm anfühlen. Einer odere mehrere Tischchen für den täglichen Gebrauch, die leicht verstellt werden können, sind ein weiterer Faktor, der einbezogen werden sollte.

libraries and studies
bibliotecas y estudios
bibliothèques et bureaux
bibliotheken und studios

LIBRARIES AND STUDIES are where books are kept, but they are also areas for reading, studying and concentration. These places should take into consideration the amount of available space and the needs of users, as they are highly personal. Different design possibilities abound, ranging from straight lines to curves, as do the materials that can be used to make them, although wood is the most common choice thanks to its elegance and warmth.

LAS BIBLIOTECAS Y ESTUDIOS sirven para resguardar libros, pero también son espacios de lectura, estudio y concentración. Es conveniente que estos sitios se adapten a las dimensiones espaciales y a las necesidades del usuario, pues son muy personales. Existen diseños de lo más variados, de líneas rectas o curvas y de una amplia gama de materiales, aunque la madera sigue siendo el material más recurrido, debido a la elegancia y calidez que brinda.

LES BIBLIOTHEQUES ET LES BUREAUX PERSONNELS sont principalement faits pour y ranger des livres mais ce sont aussi des espaces propices à la lecture, à l'étude et à la concentration. Il est donc préférable qu'ils soient de taille proportionnelle à l'ensemble des lieux et qu'ils répondent aux besoins de leurs occupants. Pièce très personnalisée, les designs proposés sont multiples pour répondre aux exigences de chacun : mobilier à ligne droite ou courbe avec une très large gamme de matériaux à disposition, bien que le bois reste celui que l'on préfère car il transforme la pièce en espace élégant et raffiné.

BIBLIOTHEKEN UND STUDIOS dienen zur Aufbewahrung von Büchern, aber es sind auch Orte zum lesen, studieren und konzentrieren. Es ist angebracht, dass diese Bereiche sich an die räumlichen Dimensionen anpassen und auch an die persönlichen Erfordernisse der Benutzer. Es gibt sehr unterschiedliche Designs mit geraden oder kurvigen Linien, sowie eine grosse Vielfalt an Materialien, obwohl Holz immernoch das am häufigsten verwendete Material ist, da es Eleganz und Wärme austrahlt.

One good way to make the most of the space in a house built on several levels is to turn certain heights of the walls into bookshelves to create a vertical library. If the floors and furnishings are made of wood, then their tones should preferably be different.

Una opción para aprovechar el espacio en una casa que tiene varias alturas es tomar los muros de remate de algunos niveles y convertirlos en libreros, creando una biblioteca vertical. Si los pisos y el mueble son de madera es preferible que difieran en tonalidad.

Avec une maison de plus d'un étage, il est possible d'utiliser les murs qui couvrent plusieurs hauteurs en bibliothèque verticale grâce à des étagères. Si les sols et les meubles sont en bois, il est préférable que les étagères de la bibliothèque soit aussi en bois mais d'une couleur différente.

Eine Alternative zur optimalen Nutzung des Platzes in einem Haus mit unterschiedlichen Deckenhöhen ist die Anbringung von Bücherregalen an einigen Abschlusswänden. Auf diese Weise entsteht eine vertikale Bibliothek. Sind die Böden und Möbel aus Holz, sollten unterschiedliche Farbtöne zur Anwendung kommen.

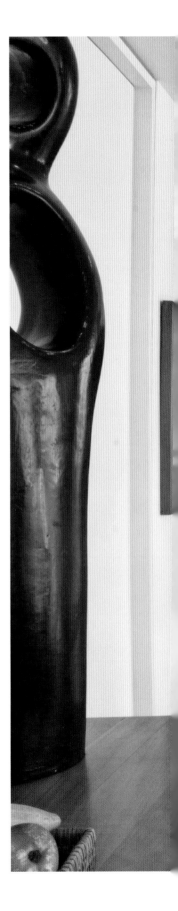

Furniture for studies and libraries has been modernized by contemporary designers, who have chosen to privilege practicality over volume and do away with carvings, moldings and inlaid work. Now furniture is simple, based on pure lines and made from very pale or very dark woods or metal and glass. These new designs have handed the dominant esthetic role to the books on the shelves, which are now part of the decoration. As a result, they can be bound in certain colors in keeping with their newly-acquired status as visual focal points.

El mobiliario para estudios y bibliotecas ha sido modernizado por los diseñadores contemporáneos, quienes han optado por restarle masividad y hacerlo más funcional, despojándolo de tallas, molduras o trabajos de marquetería. Hoy la tendencia es a incluir muebles sencillos, de líneas puras, ya sea de maderas muy claras o muy oscuras, o bien de metal y vidrio. Los nuevos diseños han llevado a que sean los libros los que protagonizan por encima de las repisas, llegando a ser parte de la decoración. Por ello, incluso se les puede forrar en determinados colores, para que sirvan de focos visuales.

Le mobilier pour les bibliothèques et les bureaux a été modernisé par les designers qui ont décidé de l'alléger et de le rendre plus fonctionnel en lui ôtant toute sculpture, moulure ou autre marqueterie. Ce sont maintenant des meubles simples, de lignes pures, en bois très clairs ou très foncés, parfois même en métal ou en verre. Les nouveaux designs laissent donc aux livres sur les étagères le premier rôle pour qu'ils deviennent eux-mêmes des éléments décoratifs. C'est pour cette raison que l'on peut envisager d'en relier certains en utilisant différentes couleurs afin d'attirer l'attention des visiteurs.

Die Möbel von Studios und Bibliotheken wurden durch die gegenwärtigen Designer modernisiert, die dazu übergehen, sie leichter und praktischer zu gestalten. Dabei wird die Grösse geringer und es finden keine Rahmen und Einlegearbeiten mehr Verwendung. Es sind einfache Möbel, die klare Linien aufweisen, wobei das Holz hell oder dunkel sein kann, oder Metall und Glas Verwendung finden. Die neuen Designs haben dazu geführt, dass die Bücher die Hauptdarsteller sind und nicht das Regal; die Bücher werden zu einem Teil der Dekoration. Daher können sie sogar mit bestimmten Farben versehen werden, damit sie zum Blickfang werden.

Outstanding results can be obtained by experimenting with different shapes and contrasting colors and by finding original ways to join one piece of furniture to another. One such option consists of curved bookshelves that swerve around the desk in a space where the dark and pale tones of the different surfaces compete with each other.

Jugar con formas, contrastar colores y vincular un mueble al otro de manera original lleva a un resultado único. Por ejemplo, una estantería curva, que abrace al escritorio de trabajo, insertados en un área donde compitan los tonos claros y oscuros de las superficies.

On peut obtenir une décoration extraordinaire si l'on sait jouer sur les formes, contraster les couleurs et associer deux meubles l'un à l'autre avec originalité. C'est le cas, par exemple, si l'on place des étagères incurvées entourant un bureau personnel dans une pièce où les surfaces de teintes claires et foncées dominent.

Das originelle Variieren von Formen, die Verwendung von Farbkontrasten und Möbeln, die untereinander in Beziehung stehen, führt zu einem einzigartigen Ergebnis.
Ein Beispiel dafür ist ein kurviges Bücherregal, das den Schreibtisch umgibt und sich in einem Bereich mit hellen und dunklen Farbtönen der Oberflächen befindet.

The imagination is the most effective tool when it comes to creating a wonderful library. Even though using wood of the same type and color throughout a space might seem excessive, an exquisite wood finish, attractive moldings, original patterns on the floor, illuminated glass cases, simple and discrete furniture blending in harmoniously with the general look of the place and a few delicate objects will generate an unbeatable esthetic effect. The bulkiness of the furniture should be in proportion with the area and an overall sense of balance must be tangible.

La imaginación es el mejor aliado para realizar una librería fascinante. Aún cuando puede pensarse que colocar madera de una misma especie y color a lo ancho y largo de un espacio puede resultar un exceso, si su acabado es fino, hay un atractivo trabajo de molduras, dibujos originales en pisos, vitrinas iluminadas, muebles que por su sobriedad y discreción actúen armónicamente con la estética general y objetos delicados el ambiente será insuperable. Es primordial que la masividad de los muebles esté proporcionada con el área y que se sienta un equilibrio integral.

L'imagination est le meilleur allié pour réaliser une belle bibliothèque. Même si l'on pense que le fait de placer des étagères d'un même bois et d'une même couleur de haut en bas et de long en large sur un mur alourdira foncièrement l'espace, si les finitions sont soignées, le résultat restera très esthétique. Avec des moulures raffinées, des motifs originaux au sol, des vitrines éclairées, un meuble sobre et discret s'inscrira harmonieusement dans la pièce et s'associera à merveille avec les objets d'art qu'on y trouve. Il est néanmoins recommandé que son importance soit proportionnelle à l'endroit pour que l'équilibre règne dans la pièce.

Mit etwas Kreativität kann ein faszinierendes Bücherregal geschaffen werden. Auch wenn Holz derselben Art und mit derselben Farbe an der Breit- und Längsseite eines Raumes übertrieben erscheinen kann, wird durch eine attraktive Zusammenstellung von Leisten, originellen Mustern auf dem Boden, die Verwendung von edlem Holz, beleuchteten Vitrinen und Möbeln, die sich durch ihre Schlichtheit und Diskretion harmonisch in die allgemeine Ästhetik einfügen, sowie raffinierte Objekte eine unübertreffliche Atmoshphäre erreicht. Es ist sehr wichtig, dass die Massivität der Möbel im richtigen Verhältnis zum Bereich steht und dass ein integrales Gleichgewicht zu spüren ist.

dining rooms and kitchens
comedores y cocinas
salles à manger et cuisines
esszimmer und küchen

DINING ROOMS ARE FOR SHARING AND SOCIALIZING, which is why they, more than any other room in the house, express the personality of its inhabitants. It is also why originality is a crucial factor. A superb option for a serene setting based on neutral materials is to use something to break the mood, such as eye-catching upholstery with organic patterns.

SIENDO ZONAS DESTINADAS A CONVIVIR Y A COMPARTIR, los comedores son los sitios de la casa que mayormente expresan la personalidad de sus habitantes, razón por la que la originalidad se convierte en un factor fundamental. En un ambiente sereno, en el que se ha optado por materiales neutros, es altamente atractivo irrumpir con algún elemento que conquiste el área; éste puede ser, por ejemplo, una atrevida tapicería con dibujos orgánicos.

ENDROITS CONÇUS POUR LA VIE EN COMMUN ET LE PARTAGE, les salles à manger sont les pièces de la maison où s'expriment le plus la personnalité des résidents et c'est pour cette raison que l'originalité y est fondamentale. Il est très séduisant et assez audacieux de rompre la sérénité de l'atmosphère tranquille, à base de tons neutres, avec ce qui deviendra l'élément-clé des lieux, par exemple, une tapisserie à motifs végétaux.

WEIL ES SICH UM EINEN BEREICH HANDELT, DER DEM Zusammenleben und dem Beisammensein dient, kommt im Esszimmer die Persönlichkeit der Bewohner besonders zum Ausdruck. Daher sollte dieser Bereich besonders originell gestaltet werden. In einer ruhigen Atmosphäre mit neutralen Materialien ist es höchst attraktiv, wenn ein Element in diesem Bereich besonders hervorgehoben wird. Hierbei kann es sich zum Beispiel um einen gewagten Bezugstoff handeln, der organische Muster aufweist.

dining rooms
comedores
salles à manger
esszimmer

If the dining room is located in a spacious, double height space, great care must be taken with the scale to make sure it is well proportioned with regard to the area. The size of the table's center also plays a decisive role in creating harmony in the room.

Si el comedor se sitúa en un espacio de doble altura y de dimensiones generosas hay que concentrar la atención en su escala para que quede lo más proporcionado con respecto al área. El tamaño del centro de mesa será también determinante para la armonía del lugar.

Si la salle à manger est de taille importante et se situe dans une pièce en double hauteur, il est nécessaire de soigner spécialement les proportions pour que tout soit à la même échelle. L'importance du centre avec la table jouera également un rôle déterminant dans l'harmonie de l'ensemble.

Steht der Esstisch in einem Bereich mit doppelter Deckenhöhe und grosszügigen Dimensionen, sollte besonders auf die Proportionen geachtet werden, damit diese so angemessen wie möglich sind. Die Grösse der Tischdekoration ist ebenfalls ausschlaggebend für die Harmonie des Ortes.

Rectangular or square dining tabletops made of Corian® or glass and set on a stainless steel base provide a sleek touch and combine well with straight-lined seating in removable smooth cotton upholstery.

Las cubiertas rectangulares o cuadradas para mesa de comedor hechas de Corian® o de vidrio, montadas sobre bases de acero inoxidable, que conservan un diseño esbelto se complementan apropiadamente con sillas de formas muy rectas con vestiduras en telas lisas de algodón, que pueden ser desfundables.

Les revêtements rectangulaires ou carrés pour tables de salle à manger Corian® ou en verre, montés sur une base en acier inoxydable, donne du mouvement au design choisi et accompagnent harmonieusement des chaises à lignes très droites recouvertes par des housses amovibles et lisses en toile de coton.

Rechteckige oder quadratische Tischplatten aus Corian® oder Glas auf Tischbeinen aus rostfreiem Edelstahl mit einem zierlichen Design, können durch Stühle mit geraden Formen und Stoffen aus unifarbener Baumwolle angemessen ergänzt werden, die abziehbare Bezüge haben können.

One foolproof way to ensure good results is to make the most of the dining room's shape. Rectangular tables, for instance, look great in long rooms. Similarly, hanging lamps whose shape mimics that of the table will light up a specific area and avoid the shadows cast by the general lighting located in the soffits. There are equally reliable options for color, such as beige and brown scales that offer an ideal way of generating a tasteful setting of distinction. The views enjoyed by diners from each seat need to be studied and defined with great care.

Aprovechar la forma del espacio en un comedor siempre lleva a resultados sin riesgo; a las estancias longitudinales les favorecen las mesas rectangulares. De igual modo, las lámparas colgantes que identifican su forma con la de la mesa iluminan el área precisa y evitan las sombras provocadas por la luz general que se ubica en plafones. En términos de color también existen opciones seguras, siendo las escalas de beiges y cafés idóneas por evocar sobriedad y distinción. Es importante estudiar y cuidar las vistas que tendrán los comensales desde cada asiento.

Profiter de la forme d'une salle à manger n'est jamais risqué. Dans les pièces tout en longueur, les tables rectangulaires s'imposent. Et des lampes suspendues, dont la forme fait écho à celle de la table, éclairent des surfaces avec précision pour que les ombres au plafond produites par la lumière générale de la pièce disparaissent. En ce qui concerne les couleurs, de nombreuses solutions sans risque existent : les beiges et les marrons, dans de nuances variées, sont parfaits pour donner à la pièce une atmosphère sobre et distinguée. Mais il est aussi important de prendre en compte et de soigner la vue que chaque invité aura une fois assis.

Wird die Form des Esszimmers eingehalten, führt dies stets zu risikolosen Ergebnissen; in länglichen Räumen sollten rechteckige Tische Verwendung finden. Gleichermassen führen Hängelampen, die der Form des Tisches folgen, zu einer präzisen Beleuchtung, bei der Schatten vermieden werden, die durch die allgemeine Deckenbeleuchtung hervorgerufen werden. In Bezug auf die Farbe gibt es ebenfalls sichere Alternativen, wie Beige- und Brauntöne, die schlicht und vornehm wirken. Es ist wichtig, die Blickwinkel zu analysieren, die die Tischgäste von jedem Stuhl aus haben.

To give the space a generous helping of vitality it is advisable to play with the light and shade, using the same raw tones for all the textiles and very dark wood for the furniture, floors and some of the walls. A hanging lamp in the form of a cascade looks very modern, while a sizeable mirror set against a dark wall will almost become a source of light in itself.

Para que el espacio exprese dinamismo se recomienda jugar con claroscuros, uniformando los textiles en tonalidades crudas y dejando el mobiliario, pisos y algún muro en madera muy oscura. Una lámpara con elementos colgantes en cascada sirve para dar el toque de modernidad y un espejo de buena escala, colocado sobre el muro oscuro, funciona como punto luminoso.

Pour donner du dynamisme à l'espace, il est conseillé de jouer sur les clairs-obscurs en harmonisant les tissus avec des tons écrus et en optant pour un bois très sombre pour le mobilier, les sols et quelques surfaces murales. Un luminaire avec des éléments suspendus en cascade donne à l'endroit une touche de modernité et un miroir proportionné aux lieux, placé sur un mur sombre, constitue une source de lumière dans la pièce.

Damit der Raum Dynamik vermittelt, sollten Hell-Dunkel-Effekte zur Anwendung kommen, wobei alle Textilien in Naturtönen gehalten und die Möbel, der Boden und eine Wand sehr dunkel gestaltet werden. Eine Lampe mit kaskadenartigen Hängeelementen verleiht einen Touch Modernität und ein grosser Spiegel, der über der dunklen Wand angebracht wird, dient als leuchtender Punkt.

One or several lamps hanging over the dining room table will afford a sensation of vitality to the space.

Una lámpara colgante o un conjunto de ellas colocadas a distintas alturas sobre la mesa del comedor le dan al espacio sensación de movimiento.

Une ou plusieurs lampes suspendues sur une table de salle à manger donne du mouvement à l'espace.

Eine oder mehrere Hängelampen über dem Esstisch verleihem dem Raum den Eindruck von Bewegung.

The style of the seats will, to a large extent, determine the overall look of the dining room and its functionality. Straight-lined seating serves both purposes, although it is especially useful for the backrest to have some kind of cushioning to make it more comfortable.

El estilo de las sillas define en buena medida tanto la estética del comedor como su funcionalidad. La sillería de líneas rectas favorece ambos aspectos, pero conviene que sus respaldos y asientos lleven algún tipo de acojinado para que sean más cómodas.

Le style choisi pour les chaises définit en grande partie l'esthétique et la fonctionnalité de la salle à manger. Opter pour des chaises à lignes droites est un plus pour ces deux domaines mais il ne faut pas oublier de garnir les dossiers et les sièges avec des revêtements en coussin pour que les chaises restent confortables.

Der Stil der Stühle definiert sowohl die Ästhetik des Esszimmers, als auch dessen Funktionalität. Stühle mit geraden Linien begünstigen beide Aspekte, obwohl es ratsam ist, dass die Rückenlehne und der Sitz gepolstert sind, weil dies bequemer ist.

A light box with onyx walls or some other sizeable architectural component can be the perfect way to mark out boundaries to separate the formal dining area from the adjoining space. In addition to this virtual frontier, it is also a good idea to differentiate the two areas by the shape of the tables, as well as their materials and surfaces. At the same time, the transition between one space and the other should not be too abrupt, which can be avoided by using the same color for the walls and ceiling.

Un elemento arquitectónico robusto, que bien puede ser una caja de luz conformada por paredes de ónix, puede funcionar perfectamente para marcar los límites y dividir la zona del comedor formal de la del antecomedor. Además de esta frontera virtual, es conveniente que los muebles de ambos sitios se diferencien incluso en las formas de la mesa, así como en sus materiales y acabados. Sin embargo, hay que poner cuidado en que la transición entre un área y la otra no sea brusca, homogenizando el color de muros y techos.

Un solide élément architectural, comme une paroi vitrée lumineuse en onyx, peut être parfait pour délimiter les espaces et séparer la salle à manger du salon. A cette frontière virtuelle, il convient d'y ajouter des meubles différents, comme des formes de table, des matériaux et des finitions distincts pour souligner la différence. Il faut toutefois soigner la transition entre les espaces pour qu'elle ne soit pas trop brusque en uniformisant la couleur des murs et des plafonds.

Ein robustes architektonisches Element, wie eine Lichtschachtel aus Onyxwänden kann perfekt zur Abgrenzung des formellen Esstisches von der Essecke dienen. Zusätzlich zu dieser visuellen Grenze ist es angebracht, dass die Möbel beider Bereiche unterschiedlich sind, und dies sogar in Bezug auf die Form des Tisches, sowie dessen Materialien und Finish. Dennoch darf der Übergang von einem Bereich in den anderen nicht brüsk sein, es sollten vielmehr die Farben der Wände und Decken homogenisiert werden.

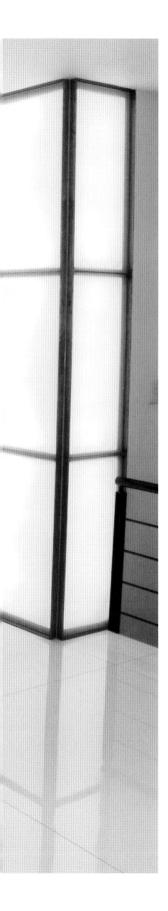

Black and white form a dramatic and highly seductive combination for a dining room. The power of these attributes can be magnified by the inclusion of a large and bright presence. The mixture of black and gray, on the other hand, is less vibrant but looks very stylish.

Negro y blanco conforman una composición drástica y altamente seductora en un comedor, aspectos que se dramatizan si se incluye un elemento luminoso, brillante y de grandes proporciones. La mezcla de negro y gris, en cambio, es menos vibrante pero evoca elegancia.

L'association du noir et du blanc est esthétique et très efficace dans une salle à manger et on peut rehausser les effets produits avec un luminaire de forte intensité et de grande taille. En revanche, combiner le noir et le gris capte moins l'attention mais donne de l'élégance à la pièce.

Schwarz und weiss sind eine drastische Zusammenstellung, die an einem Esstisch höchst verführerisch wirkt. Diese Aspekte werden noch dramatisiert, wenn ein leuchtendes, glänzendes und grossflächiges Element zur Anwendung kommt. Die Mischung von schwarz und grau ist weniger auffällig, wirkt aber sehr elegant.

A dividing wall located between the two most important social areas of the house – the lounge and dining room – must be esthetically and structurally sound. This can be achieved by using some type of stone, such as onyx, whose yellowish tones come to life when illuminated. To make this element really stand out, the best bet is to try out different plane arrangements using a longer, bare concrete wall, with unquestionable vitality but neutral in its coloring. Light brown floors and furnishings are a great complement for this decoration.

Se antoja que un muro divisorio ubicado entre las zonas públicas más importantes de la casa –sala y comedor– posea fuerza estética y tectónica. Una alternativa para lograrlo es construirlo en algún material pétreo, como el ónix, cuyo tono amarillento se estimula cuando está iluminado. Es posible que este elemento adquiera mayor interés espacial si juega en planos con otro muro de mayor longitud, de concreto aparente, cuya energía es evidente pero su colorido es neutro. Pisos y muebles de madera castaña van bien con esta decoración.

On souhaite souvent que la paroi de séparation entre les deux espaces communs les plus importants de la maison (le salon et la salle à manger) ait une forte présence esthétique et architecturale. Opter pour un matériau pierreux, comme l'onyx dont les tons jaunes ressortent sous l'effet de la lumière, est un bon moyen d'y parvenir. Et il est possible de souligner la présence de cette séparation dans l'espace en jouant sur les surfaces planes avec un mur de plus grande proportion, en béton apparent et de couleur neutre, mais au dynamisme certain. Des sols et des meubles en châtaignier iront merveilleusement bien avec cette décoration.

Eine Trennwand zwischen den wichtigsten öffentlichen Bereichen des Hauses -Wohnzimmer und Esszimmer- sollte ästhetische und tektonische Stärke aufweisen. Eine Alternative ist es, diese Wand aus einem Steinmaterial zu fertigen, wie Onyx, dessen gelblicher Farbton bei Beleuchtung stimuliert wird. Es ist möglich, dass dieses Element noch interessanter im Raum wirkt, wenn eine weitere, noch längere Wand aus sichtbarem Beton vorhanden ist, die Energie ausstrahlt, während die Farbe neutral ist. Böden und Möbel aus kastanienbraunem Holz passen gut zu dieser Dekoration.

A table made of wooden slats combines wonderfully with seats made of natural fibers like wicker or reed. The tone should ideally be dark red or brown to generate a contrast.

Una mesa de tablones de madera maciza se integra estupendo con sillas de fibras naturales como el mimbre o el bejuco; conviene que su tono sea rojizo oscuro o chocolate para provocar contraste.

Une table en bois massif est parfaite si on y associe des chaises en fibres naturelles comme l'osier ou le rotin mais il est préférable qu'elle soit de couleur rougeâtre et foncée ou chocolat pour qu'il y ait contraste.

Ein Tisch aus massiven Holzplanken kombiniert hervorragend mit Stühlen aus Naturfasern, wie Rattan oder Schilf; ein dunkler, rötlicher oder brauner Farbton ist geeignet, um Kontraste zu schaffen.

kitchens
cocinas
cuisines
küchen

MODERN-DAY KITCHENS are where esthetic design, technology and contemporary shapes join forces in a single space, as well as practical and useful. The best materials for providing these qualities and ensuring harmonious interaction are stone, stainless steel, aluminum and glass. Their neutrality means they combine very well with wooden furniture with a matt, semi-gloss or gloss finish. When stone is used, it should be a single component to make sure it looks good and is easy to clean.

LAS COCINAS ACTUALES fusionan en su diseño estética, tecnología y formas modernas, además de ser prácticas y útiles. La gama de materiales que mejor conjunta dichas características y actúa armónicamente en el espacio son piedra, acero inoxidable, aluminio y vidrio; su carga neutra hace que se puedan mezclar maravillosamente con muebles de madera en acabados mate, semi-brillante o lustroso. Si se usan piedras hay que procurar que sean de una sola pieza, pues lucen espectaculares y son de fácil limpieza.

LE DESIGN DES CUISINES ACTUELLES prend aussi bien en compte l'esthétique, la technologie et les formes modernes que le côté pratique et utile de cette pièce. La gamme des matériaux utilisés pour parvenir à respecter ses caractéristiques et harmoniser l'espace comprend la pierre, l'acier inoxydable, l'aluminium et le verre. Leur poids neutre dans la décoration fait qu'ils peuvent être associés avec des meubles en bois comportant des finitions mates, semi-brillantes ou brillantes. Si on utilise la pierre, il est préférable qu'elle se présente en une seule pièce, car son apparence n'en sera que plus esthétique et elle sera facile à entretenir.

DIE AKTUELLEN KÜCHEN vereinen in ihrem Design Ästhetik, Technik und modern Formen und sind ausserdem praktisch und nützlich. Die Materialien, die diese Eigenschaften am besten verbinden und harmonisch im Raum zusammenwirken sind Stein, rostfreier Edelstahl, Aluminium und Glas; ihre Neutralität führt dazu, dass sie wunderbar mit Möbeln aus Holz mit matter, halbglänzender oder glänzender Oberfläche kombiniert werden können. Werden Steine verwendet, sollte es sich um ein einziges Stück handeln, denn dies sieht spektakulär aus und ist einfach zu reinigen.

In a long undivided area that houses the living room, dining
room and kitchen, it is a good idea to include features
that will highlight the unity of the space. This effect can
be achieved by choosing a few colors and materials to
harmonize the floor or ceiling.

En una estancia corrida y sin divisiones, donde comparten
el espacio sala, cocina y comedor, conviene que existan
elementos que hagan sentir al espacio como una unidad;
esto se logra limitando la selección a unos cuantos colores
y materiales, y unificando el piso o el techo.

Avec une pièce ouverte et sans divisions où l'on trouve le
salon, la cuisine et la salle à manger, il est conseillé d'y placer
des éléments qui uniformisent l'espace dans son entier.
On peut y parvenir en se limitant à quelques couleurs et à
quelques matériaux et en harmonisant le sol et le plafond.

In einem durchgehenden Wohnraum ohne Abgrenzungen,
wo sich in einem Raum das Wohnzimmer, die Küche und das
Esszimmer befinden, sollten Elemente vorhanden sein, die den
Eindruck einer Einheit verstärken; dabei kann es sich um die
Wahl von wenigen Farben und Materialien handeln, wobei
ferner der Boden oder die Decke einheitlich sein sollten.

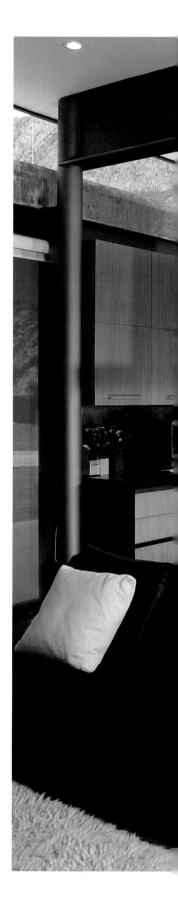

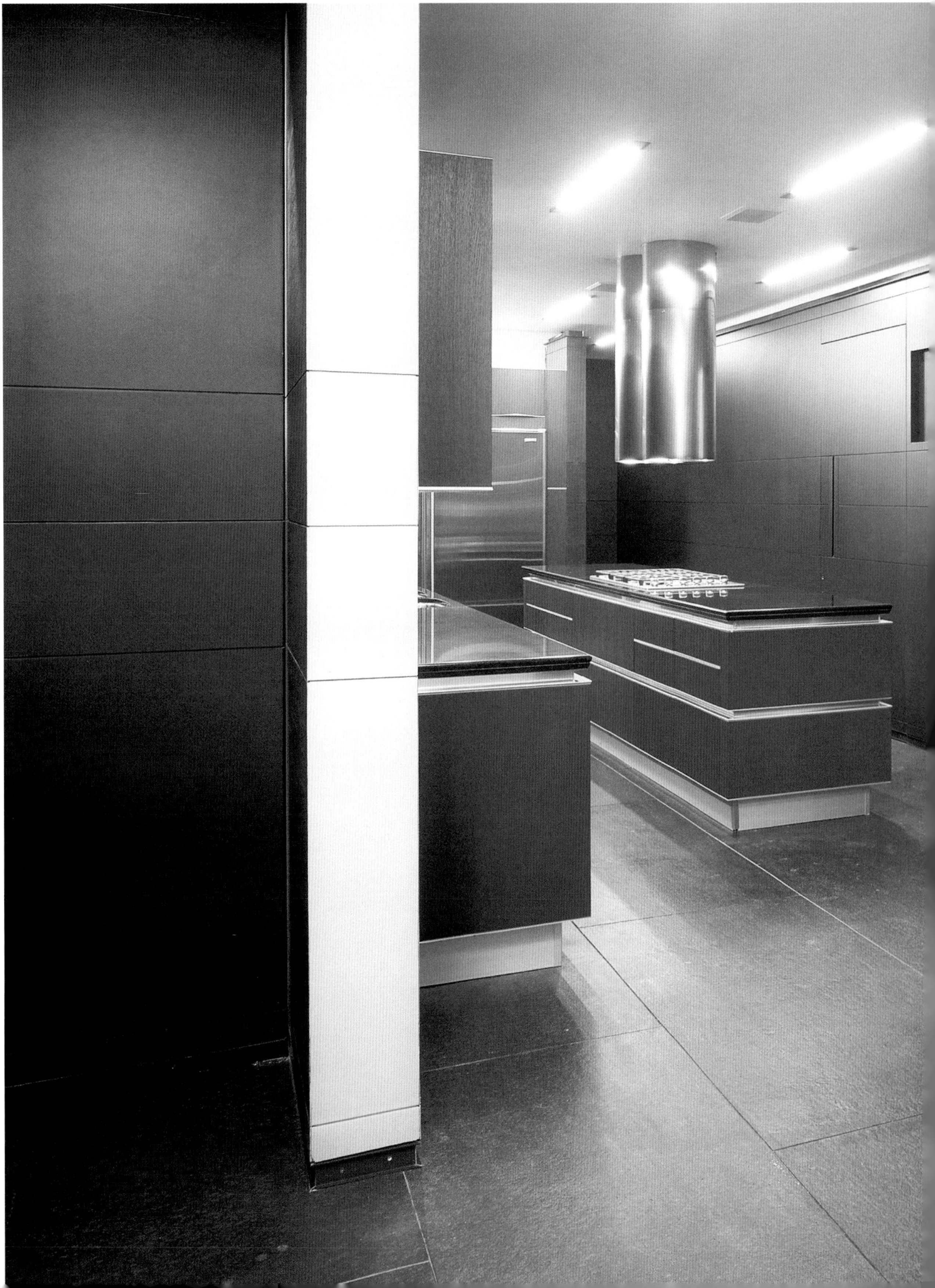

A couple of half moon lamps at the center of the isle will make the isle stand out visually. The area will therefore not be plunged into darkness by shadows cast by the lights in the soffits, making it more practical for preparing, chopping and decorating the dishes bound for the dining room.

Colocar dos lámparas en forma de media luna al centro de la isla permite mejorar la visibilidad en la misma. Esta zona funcionará bien para cortar, picar y decorar los platos que van al comedor, pues no se verá afectada por las sombras que proyecten las luminarias ubicadas en plafones.

Placer deux lampes en forme de demi-lune au-dessus d'un plan de travail au centre de la cuisine est un bon moyen d'améliorer la visibilité. L'endroit n'en sera que plus commode pour pouvoir y couper, hacher et décorer des plats ou des ingrédients qui prennent la direction de la salle à manger car l'ombre projetée par les luminaires au plafond ne sera pas gênante.

Werden in der Mitte der Insel zwei Lampen mit Halbmondform angebracht, so ermöglicht dies eine bessere Sicht. Dieser Bereich ist zum Schneiden, Zerkleidern und Dekorieren von Gerichten geeignet, die dann in das Esszimmer gebracht werden, denn hier besteht keine Beeinträchtigung durch die Schatten, die durch die Beleuchtung in der abgehängten Decke verursacht werden.

A kitchen's most crucial attributes include cleanliness, tidiness and hygiene. Pure white furnishings and surfaces combine exquisitely with stainless steel and glass to create a sensation of orderliness, especially if the walls are also painted white. The same effect can be achieved through the substantial presence of stainless steel. The inclusion of metals and smooth surfaces will add a sparkle to the kitchen, turning it into a magically brilliant place.

Entre las características imprescindibles en una cocina se encuentran la limpieza, el orden y la higiene. El mobiliario y las cubiertas de color blanco puro, en combinación con el acero inoxidable y el vidrio generan la impresión de nitidez, sobre todo si los muros también están pintados de blanco. El mismo efecto se consigue con el dominio del acero inoxidable. La introducción de metales y superficies lisas en la decoración de esta zona provoca destellos y brillos imprimiéndole al sitio un toque mágico y realzando su resplandor.

Il est indispensable qu'une cuisine soit propre, en ordre et que l'hygiène y soit respectée. Un mobilier et des revêtements blanc pur, associés à de l'acier inoxydable et à du verre, donnent à la pièce un aspect net et propre, en particulier si les murs sont également de couleur blanche. On peut aussi obtenir cette impression lorsque l'acier inoxydable domine l'endroit. L'utilisation de métaux et de surfaces lisses dans la décoration de la cuisine la font briller et scintiller pour en faire un espace magique et splendide.

Unter den unabdingbaren Eigenschaften einer Küche befinden sich Reinheit, Ordnung und Hygiene. Die Möbel und die Oberflächen aus purem Weiss, in Verbingung mit rostfreiem Edelstahl und Glas erwecken den Eindruck von Schärfe, vor allem wenn die Wände auch weiss gestrichen sind. Der gleiche Effekt wird erzielt, wenn rostfreier Edelstahl vorherrscht. Die Einführung von Metallen und glatten Oberflächen in Bezug auf die Dekoration dieses Bereiches verursacht Glitzern und Glänzen, wobei dem Bereich ein magischer Touch verliehen und dessen Glanz noch hervorgehoben wird.

Kitchen furniture is based on straight lines and pure shapes for matters of practicality and ergonomics, as well as due to current trends in design. This makes it necessary to pay special attention to the shapes of the extractors, handles and faucets to make sure they perform an effective ornamental role.

Tanto por cuestión de practicidad y ergonomía como por tendencia de diseño, el mobiliario de cocina es de líneas rectas y formas puras; esta situación conduce a poner especial cuidado en las formas de las campanas extractoras, en las agarraderas y los grifos, los cuales se convierten en elementos decorativos.

Parce qu'il se doit d'être pratique, parce que l'endroit doit être une pièce accueillante et pour suivre les dernières tendances en matière de décoration, le mobilier d'une cuisine comporte en général des lignes droites et des formes pures. Il est donc important de bien choisir la forme de la hotte, des poignées et des robinets pour en faire aussi des éléments décoratifs.

Sowohl aus praktischen Gründen und im Hinblick auf die Ergonomie, als auch aufgrund der Designtrends, weisen die Möbel in der Küche gerade Linien und pure Formen auf; diese Situation erfordert es, dass der Form der Abzugshaube, den Griffen und Wasserhähnen besondere Aufmerksamkeit zukommen, die sich in dekorative Elemente verwandeln.

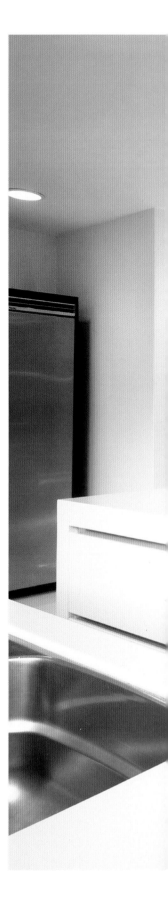

It is generally advisable to use the perimeter walls for the positioning of kitchen furniture and leave as much space as possible free. This space will be further enriched by opening up a view on some greenery.

Aún cuando es recomendable utilizar los perímetros para adosar a ellos los muebles de cocina y generar la mayor área de movilidad posible, abrir alguna vista hacia el verde enriquece el espacio.

Même s'il est recommandé d'utiliser les contours de la pièce pour y placer les meubles de la cuisine et profiter au mieux des dimensions de l'endroit, une ouverture avec une fenêtre qui donne sur la nature éclatante embellit l'espace.

Auch wenn es empfehlenswert ist, die Wände zu nutzen, um an ihnen die Küchenmöbel zu befestigen und den grösstmöglichen Bereich frei zu halten, wird der Raum auch durch den Blick ins Grüne bereichert.

Polished stone surfaces are non-porous, which means they are hygienic and easy to clean.

Las cubiertas de piedra muy pulida facilitan la limpieza y son higiénicas, pues sus poros están muy cerrados.

Les revêtements en pierre soigneusement polie facilitent l'entretien de la pièce et sont très hygiéniques, leurs pores étant très serrés.

Oberflächen aus sehr poliertem Stein erleichtern die Reinigung und sind hygienisch, denn die Poren sind besonders geschlossen.

The specific qualities of the furniture and wall finishes in the kitchen can be brought out to the full by creating a contrast between them. This effect can be further enhanced by using contrasting colors, textures, brilliances and reflections.

Provocando el contraste deliberado entre los acabados de los muebles y los muros de la cocina se consigue que se resalten las características particulares de cada uno de ellos. Para dramatizar el efecto se deben tomar en cuenta contrastes de color, texturas, brillos y reflejos.

Si l'on veut parvenir à créer un contraste entre les finitions des meubles et les murs de la cuisine, il est nécessaire de faire ressortir les caractéristiques de ces deux éléments. Pour que l'effet soit réussi, on devra prendre en compte les contrastes existant entre les couleurs, les textures, les éclats et les reflets.

Wird ein Kontrast zwischen den Möbeln und den Wänden der Küche geschaffen, führt dies dazu, dass die Eigenschaften beider Bereiche hervorgehoben werden. Zum Dramatisieren des Effektes sind die Kontraste von Farbe, Textur, Glanz und Reflexen zu berücksichtigen.

bathrooms and bedrooms
baños y dormitorios
salles de bain et chambres à coucher
badezimmer und schlafzimmer

bathrooms baños salles de bain badezimmer

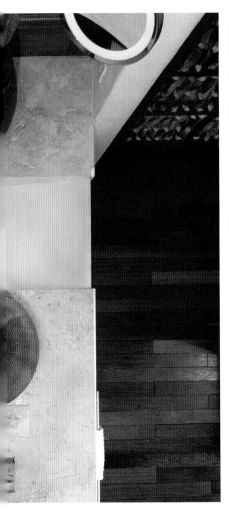

The area for personal hygiene is ideal for applying a few good decorative touches. Trying out different options with the yellow tones of onyx or dyeing sections of the stone in the same tone create the impression of freshness.

El área de lavabo se presta a ser decorada. Jugando con el amarillo del ónix o tiñendo partes de la piedra en el mismo tono se alcanza la sensación de frescura.

L'endroit où se trouve le lavabo se prête à la décoration. En jouant sur la couleur jaune de l'onyx ou en teintant certaines parties de la pierre dans le même ton, on donne à la salle de bain une sensation de fraîcheur.

Der Bereich des Waschbeckens eignet sich gut für Dekorationszwecke. Durch das Gelb des Onyx und die Färbung eines Bereiches des Steines mit demselben Farbton, wird der Eindruck von Frische erweckt.

THANKS TO BREAKTHROUGHS IN TECHNOLOGY and the arrival of new materials there is now a whole range of bathroom furniture available on the market. Bathtubs in particular have undergone major changes, including their very morphology. Some of them are oval on the outside, echoing the contours of washbasins, while on the inside they evoke the feeling of being in a watery womb.

GRACIAS A LOS AVANCES DE LA TECNOLOGÍA y al surgimiento de nuevos materiales, hoy existe en el mercado una amplia gama de muebles para baño. Particularmente las tinas han tenido cambios trascendentes, incluyendo sus morfologías. Algunas de ellas se caracterizan por seguir en su exterior formas ovaladas que evocan a las de los lavabos, en tanto que al interior provocan que quien las usa se sienta como si estuviera adentro de una matriz acuosa.

GRACE AUX AVANCEES DE LA TECHNOLOGIE et à l'arrivée de nouveaux matériaux, le marché aujourd'hui propose un grand choix de meubles pour salle de bain. Les baignoires ont énormément changé, en particulier leur forme. Certaines ont des formes extérieures ovales et font penser aux lavabos alors qu'à l'intérieur on a l'impression d'être lové dans un fauteuil « matrice » aux eaux protectrices.

DANK DEM TECHNISCHEN FORTSCHRITT und der Verwendung neuer Materialien, gibt es heutzutage auf dem Markt eine grosse Vielfalt an Badezimmermöbeln. Besonders die Badewannen haben grosse Veränderungen erfahren, ihre Form mit inbegriffen. Einige weisen im Äusseren weiterhin ovale Formen auf, die an Waschbecken erinnern, während sie im Inneren so ausgestattet sind, dass der Benutzer sich darin besonders wohlfühlt.

Transparent and translucent objects can be used to subdivide different areas of the bathroom without interrupting its visual continuity.

La utilización de elementos transparentes y translúcidos permite subdividir las distintas zonas del baño sin interrumpir la continuidad visual.

Utiliser des éléments transparents et translucides permet de diviser la salle de bain en différents espaces sans en interrompre la continuité visuelle.

Die Verwendung von durchsichtigen und transparenten Elementen ermöglicht die Unterteilung von verschiedenen Bereichen des Bades, ohne dass dadurch die visuelle Kontinuität gestört wird.

Bathrooms can be functional and cozy at the same time. A vital factor in ensuring this is to make sure the walls and floors have smooth, easy-to-clean and attractive surfaces. Stone and wood are particularly good candidates, because they allow bulky volumes to be installed easily with relatively few joints. When it comes to washbasins, it is a good idea to try out different original designs and materials, provided the platform or cabinet are on an appropriate scale for the basin.

Los baños pueden ser funcionales y acogedores al mismo tiempo. Para conseguirlo es necesario que los recubrimientos de sus muros y pisos sean de materiales duraderos, de sencilla limpieza y atractivos; la piedra o la madera resultan especialmente interesantes, pues permiten piezas de grandes formatos que facilitan su instalación con un reducido número de juntas. En cuanto a los lavabos, es importante experimentar con diseños originales y jugar con los materiales asegurando que la plataforma o gabinete esté de acuerdo con la escala del lavamanos.

Pour qu'une salle de bain soit à la fois pratique et confortable, il est nécessaire de recouvrir les murs et les sols avec des matériaux esthétiques, solides et faciles à nettoyer. La pierre et le bois sont particulièrement indiqués pour y parvenir car ils peuvent se présenter sous la forme de pièces de grande taille qu'il sera facile de poser et qui nécessiteront peu de raccords. Quant aux lavabos, il est important d'essayer des designs originaux et de jouer sur les matériaux tout en s'assurant que les étagères ou le meuble de la salle de bain soit à l'échelle de l'ensemble.

Badezimmer können zugleich praktisch und gemütlich sein. Um dies zu erreichen ist es nötig, dass die Oberflächen der Wände und Böden ein haltbares Material aufweisen, die leicht zu reinigen und attraktiv sind. Stein und Holz sind besonders interessant, da hier grosse Stücke installiert werden können, die nur wenige Fugen aufweisen. Bei den Waschbecken sollte mit originellen Designs experimentiert und die Materialien variiert werden, wobei stets darauf zu achten ist, dass der Waschtisch oder der Unterschrank mit der Grösse des Waschbeckens übereinstimmen.

It is useful to differentiate between the daily usage bathroom and the one for guests, which should be impeccable in appearance. Monochromatic decorations in gray, black or any other dark tone look stylish and refined, but they run the risk of being monotonous. This fine dividing line between a relaxed setting and a boring room can be satisfactorily negotiated by adding texture and including something in pale colors, which could be the washbasin. Stainless steel fittings and silver-colored mirrors are an excellent complement for these ambiences.

Es conveniente diferenciar el baño de uso diario del de visitas; este último es también llamado de cortesía, razón por la cual debe lucir impecable. Las decoraciones monocromas en grises, negros o cualquier otro tono oscuro son elegantes y refinadas, pero corren el riesgo de parecer monótonas. Para romper esta fina frontera entre un ambiente tranquilo y un espacio aburrido es suficiente con añadir textura e introducir un elemento de color claro, que bien puede ser el lavabo. Los accesorios en acero inoxidable y los espejos plateados complementan bien estas atmósferas.

Il est conseillé de bien faire la différence entre la salle de bain que l'on utilise tous les jours et celle réservée aux visites. Par visite, on se réfère souvent aux amis et il est donc important de soigner l'apparence de cette dernière. Les décorations monochromes, grises, noires ou de tout autre couleur foncée, font de la pièce un endroit élégant et raffiné mais risquent d'affadir un peu les lieux. Pour éviter que cet endroit calme soit vu comme ennuyeux, il suffit d'y ajouter du tissu et une couleur claire, par exemple pour le lavabo. Et les accessoires en acier inoxydable et les miroirs argentés parachèvent à merveille ce genre de décoration.

Das Gästebad sollte anders gestaltet werden als das Bad, das täglich benutzt wird. Ersteres steht den Besuchern zur Verfügung und sollte stets einwandfrei sein. Monochrome Dekorationen in grau, schwarz oder einem anderen dunklen Farbton, sind elegant und raffiniert, es besteht jedoch die Gefahr, dass sie monoton wirken. Um diese feine Grenze zwischen einer ruhigen Atmosphäre und einem langweiligen Ort zu durchbrechen ist es ausreichend, Textur und Elemente in hellen Farbtönen hinzuzufügen, wobei es sich zum Beispiel um das Waschbecken handeln kann. Accesoires aus rostfreiem Edelstahl und silberne Spiegel ergänzen diese Atmosphären auf angemessene Art und Weise.

Venetian mosaics are still widely used on bathroom walls, thanks to their attractive and modern designs in ceramics, marble or glass.

El mosaico veneciano sigue siendo utilizado como recubrimiento de muros en baños ya que con sus pequeñas piezas cerámicas, de mármol o de vidrio, se consiguen diseños estéticos y muy modernos.

On continue d'utiliser la mosaïque vénitienne pour recouvrir les murs des salles de bain car, avec ses petits fragments de céramique, de marbre ou de verre, il est possible de créer des designs aussi bien esthétiques que très modernes.

Mosaikkacheln finden nach wie vor Verwendung zur Verkleidung von Wänden in Badezimmern, denn die kleinen Stücke aus Keramik, Marmor oder Glas ermöglichen ästhetische und sehr moderne Designs.

Stone is not only structurally strong as a material but also offers a range of tones and textures, making a combination of different types of stone a great way to arrange and define different areas of the bathroom. A touch of color on the base of the washbasin and the fittings is never off the target.

Los materiales pétreos no sólo exhiben su fuerza tectónica sino también sus distintos matices y texturas, por lo que la combinación de piedras es una solución que permite organizar y delimitar distintas áreas en el baño. El toque de color puede ir en la base del lavamanos y en accesorios.

Les matériaux en pierre présentent non seulement une apparence solide mais également des couleurs et des textures différentes. En les utilisant sous plusieurs formes, on peut donc aménager la salle de bain et procéder à des séparations. Et on peut opter pour une touche de couleur en particulier avec la base du lavabo ou certains accessoires.

Steinmaterialien stellen nicht nur ihre tektonische Stärke zur Schau, sondern auch ihre unterschiedlichen Farbnuancen und Texturen. Daher ist die Kombination mit Stein eine Lösung, die die Organisation und Abgrenzung von verschiedenen Bereichen des Bades ermöglicht. Die Basis des Waschtisches und die Accesoires können einen Touch Farbe aufweisen.

A bathroom should look like a place of rest and relaxation, so it is preferable not to use too many colors and finishes. Keeping the bathroom fairly neutral in this respect will increase its "feel good" factor. However, this does not mean that the decorative contribution should be disregarded. Far from it, a focal point should be defined to adorn the space or infuse it with character; it could be anything from a whole illuminated wall to a sequence of burning candles.

Se antoja que la apariencia de un baño invite al relajamiento y al descanso, por ello es relevante que no se incluya una gama abundante de acabados y colores; cuanto más neutral sea este espacio, tanto mejor será la sensación al estar en él. Ello no implica, sin embargo, que se excluya la parte decorativa. Por el contrario, marcar un punto focal que dote de personalidad al espacio o funcione como detalle es altamente recomendable y éste puede ser desde un muro completo iluminado hasta una serie de velas encendidas.

L'atmosphère d'une salle de bain doit inviter à la détente et au repos. Il est donc recommandé de limiter le nombre de finitions et de couleurs. Plus la pièce est neutre et plus on aimera y rester. Ceci ne veut toutefois pas dire que l'on doit y négliger la décoration. Au contraire, une touche de lumière personnalisera l'espace et deviendra l'élément-clé de la pièce. Un mur entièrement éclairé, voire plusieurs bougies allumées, sont des détails particulièrement conseillés pour y parvenir.

Das Badezimmer sollte zum Entspannen und Erholen einladen, daher ist es wichtig, dass keine grosse Vielfalt an Oberflächen und Farben verwendet wird. Je neutraler der Raum gehalten wird, desto wohler fühlt man sich darin. Das bedeutet nicht, dass der dekorative Part keine Anwendung findet. Ganz im Gegenteil, ein Blickfang, der dem Raum Persönlichkeit verleiht oder Details sind höchst empfehlenswert. Dabei kann es sich um eine komplett beleuchtete Wand handeln oder eine Reihe brennender Kerzen.

Wood looks great on walls and, in the case of bathrooms, can even offer highly original solutions because it has not been explored exhaustively by designers yet. If the wood is hard and correctly treated, it will be perfectly damp proof, especially if it is placed away from damp areas. Metal bathroom fittings are visually very appealing when combined with wood and may be shaped to provide outstanding adornments.

Una aplicación muy lucidora de la madera es sobre muros; en el caso particular de los baños esta solución es inclusive original, pues ha sido poco explotada por los diseñadores. Si la madera es dura y está bien tratada resiste perfectamente la humedad y sobre todo si se le coloca lejos del área húmeda. Los accesorios metálicos para baño se ven estupendos en conjunto con la madera y según sus formas se pueden posar en el espacio como piezas decorativas sobresalientes.

Recouvrir des murs avec du bois est à la fois très judicieux et très original pour une salle de bain car peu de designers y ont pensé jusqu'à présent. Si le bois est dur et bien traité, il résistera parfaitement à l'humidité, en particulier si on le place loin des endroits humides. Les accessoires en métal pour salle de bain vont remarquablement bien avec le bois et leurs différentes formes font qu'ils peuvent également être utilisés comme d'importants objets décoratifs.

Wird Holz auf Wänden angebracht, führt dies zu einem attraktiven Effekt. Im Falle von Badezimmern ist diese Lösung auch noch originell, denn dieses Vorgehen wird von den Designern wenig genutzt. Ist das Holz hart und gut behandelt, widersteht es perfekt der Feuchtigkeit, dennoch sollte es in gewissem Abstand zu den Feuchtzonen angebracht werden. Metallene Accesoires im Bad sehen zusammen mit dem Holz hervorragend aus und in Abhängigkeit von den Formen können sie im Raum wie dekorative Stücke wirken.

Floral patterns, along with a number of other designs printed on vinyl, look very good on bathroom walls and furniture. If they are very eye-catching, then all the other elements present should stand out for their neutrality, to which end glass with its different finishes is ideal.

Los patrones florales así como muchos otros diseños estampados en vinilo lucen bien en muebles y muros de baños. Si son muy llamativos hay que procurar que el resto de los elementos se distinga por su neutralidad, el vidrio en sus diversos acabados es ideal para este fin.

Beaucoup de motifs imprimés sur du vinyle, comme des fleurs, conviennent bien aux meubles et aux murs des salles de bain. S'ils attirent énormément le regard, il est nécessaire de soigner la neutralité des autres éléments en utilisant, par exemple, du verre qui, qu'elle que soit la finition employée, est idéal pour y parvenir.

Blumenmuster wie auch viele andere Designs auf Vinyl auf Möbeln und Wänden im Badezimmer sehen attraktiv aus. Sind sie sehr auffällig, sollte der Rest der vorhandenen Elemente neutral sein. Glas in seinen verschiedenen Ausführungen ist ideal für diesem Zweck.

Some interior designers prefer ovaline basins to the more classical variants. The most commonly used materials today range from glass to porcelain. Either way, chrome faucets and fittings are always an attractive option.

Algunos interioristas prefieren los ovalines en vez de los clásicos lavamanos; las tendencias en cuanto a materiales abarcan desde el vidrio hasta la porcelana. En cualquier caso la grifería y accesorios cromados lucen estupendos.

Aux lavabos de forme traditionnelle, certains décorateurs préfèrent ceux de forme ovale. Quant aux dernières tendances en ce qui concerne leurs matériaux, cela va du verre à la porcelaine. Quoi qu'il en soit, la robinetterie et les accessoires chromés vont remarquablement bien avec l'ensemble.

Einige Innendekorateure bevorzugen aufgesetze anstelle von klassischen Waschbecken. Die Trends in Bezug auf die Materialien gehen von Glas bis Porzellan. In jedem Fall sehen chromfarbene Wasserhähne und Accesoires hervorragend aus.

When there is enough space, the bathtub area can be separated from the shower area by glass walls to allow visual continuity. The boundary between one area and the other can be marked by using different floor surfaces.

Si el espacio lo permite, es muy cómodo tener dividida la zona de tina de la de regadera y hacer los cerramientos con muros de vidrio para fomentar la continuidad visual. El límite entre una zona y otra se puede marcar cambiando el acabado del piso.

Si l'espace est assez grand, il est pratique de séparer la douche de la baignoire mais avec des parois en verre pour préserver la continuité visuelle de la pièce. Et il est possible de souligner la séparation entre les deux zones avec des sols différents.

Wenn der Platz dies erlaubt ist es sehr bequem, wenn der Bereich der Badewanne von der Dusche abgetrennt wird. Die Unterteilung wird durch Glaswände vorgenommen, damit die visuelle Kontinuität nicht gestört wird. Die Grenze zwischen einem Bereich und dem anderen kann durch eine andere Art von Boden markiert werden.

Basins can be square, rectangular, circular or oval, as well as fixed to the wall or placed on top of an item of furniture, but, regardless of their shape and location, they play a key role in determining what the bathroom looks like. It is also a good idea to make sure the place they stand in is well-lit and, preferably, enjoys the embellishing presence of a mirror. This effect could also be provided with a vase or by painting the wall the mirror is fixed to.

Cuadrados, rectangulares, redondos u ovalados; colocados sobre una cubierta, empotrados a muro o puestos sobre un gabinete, los lavamanos se han convertido en piezas clave para la estética del baño y tienen mucho que ver con el aspecto general del mismo. En cualquier versión que se elija es importante que el área donde se ubiquen quede iluminada y que de preferencia cuente con un espejo embellecedor. El toque se puede obtener con un florero o pintando el muro que soporta al espejo.

Carrés, rectangulaires, ronds ou de forme ovale, les lavabos sont devenus des éléments-clés pour l'esthétique de la salle de bain et définissent pratiquement cette dernière, qu'ils soient fixés sur une surface plane, sur un meuble ou suspendus. Quelle que soit l'option choisie, il est important de les placer dans des endroits bien éclairés et de préférence face à un miroir qui le mettra en valeur. En ajoutant un vase dans la pièce ou en peignant le mur qui supporte le miroir, on rehausse l'esthétique de la décoration.

Quadratisch, rechteckig, rund oder oval; auf einem Waschtisch angebracht, in die Wand eingelassen oder auf einem Möbel: die Waschbecken haben sich in das entscheidende Stück für die Ästhetik des Badezimmers verwandelt und haben grossen Einfluss auf das allgemeine Erscheinungsbild dieses Raumes. Gleichgültig welche Version gewählt wird, ist es wichtig, dass der Bereich der Waschbecken gut beleuchtet ist und dass dort vorzugsweise ein schöner Spiegel angebracht wird. Ein besonderer Touch kann durch Verwendung einer Vase oder Bemalen der Wand erzielt werden, an der der Spiegel hängt.

One interesting design variant is to house the washbasin and dressing areas in the same space, using the furniture the washbasin sits on to insert drawers and a few extra places for storage. Wood can be used to harmonize the appearance of the space and create a pleasant contrast with stone.

Una interesante opción de diseño es que el área de lavabos y el vestidor compartan espacio, aprovechando el gabinete que soporta al lavamanos para colocar cajoneras y algunas plazas extras para almacenado. Para unificar la estética se sugiere usar madera y hacerla contrastar con la piedra.

Associer les lavabos au dressing est intéressant en matière de design. L'élément unificateur sera dans ce cas le meuble sur lequel sont fixés les lavabos, meuble que l'on dotera de tiroirs et qui sera de taille suffisante pour pouvoir y ranger ce que l'on souhaite. Autre élément esthétique unificateur : un bois qui contraste avec la pierre

Eine interessante Designalternative ist die Kombination von Waschbecken und Ankleidezimmer im selben Raum. Das Möbel, auf dem die Waschbecken ruhen wird dabei zum Anbringen von Schubladen und für sonstige Bereiche zum Aufbewahren genutzt. Zur Vereinigung der Ästhetik ist es empfehlenswert, Holz zu verwenden und mit Stein einen Kontrast zu setzen.

One of the more distinguished simple and pure-lined furniture bathroom options is the Japanese bathtub made entirely of wood and deeper than the more common tubs. One benefit of wood is that it keeps the temperature of water steady for a long time.

Entre los muebles de baño de líneas simples y puras, destaca por su diseño la tina estilo japonés hecha totalmente en madera y con una profundidad mayor a la de las tinas comunes. La madera ofrece la ventaja de conservar la temperatura del agua por largo tiempo.

Parmi les meubles aux lignes simples et pures, on remarquera le design de la baignoire de style japonais totalement en bois et dont la profondeur est plus importante que celle des baignoires ordinaires. De plus, le bois possède l'avantage de conserver la température de l'eau très longtemps.

Unter den Badezimmermöbeln mit einfachen, reinen Linien befindet sich die Badewanne im japanischen Stil, die vollständig aus Holz gefertigt ist und tiefer als die gewöhnlichen Badewannen ist. Das Holz bietet den Vorteil, dass es die Wassertemperatur über einen langen Zeitraum beibehält.

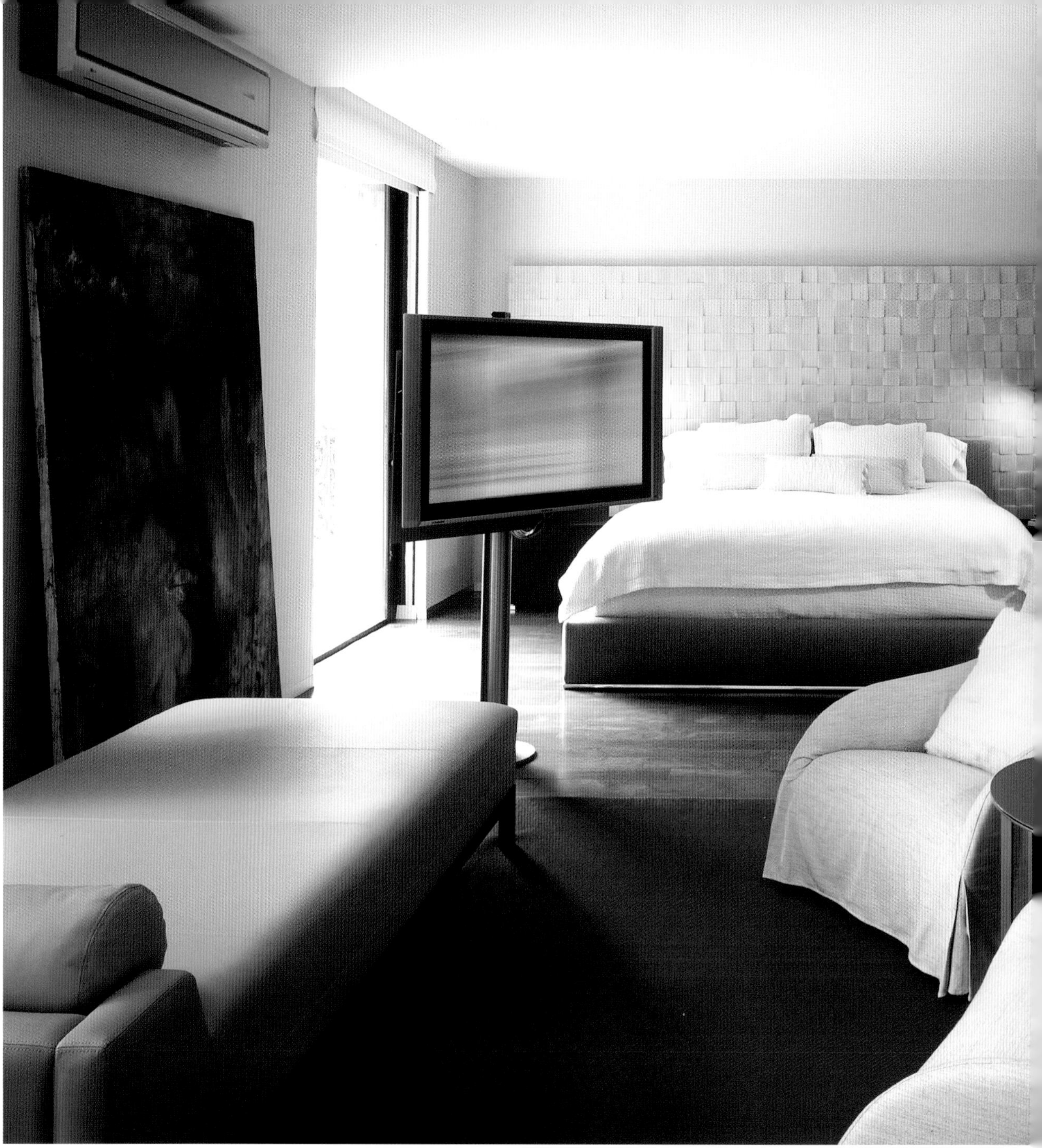

bedrooms
dormitorios
chambres à coucher
schlafzimmer

THE DESIGN OF EACH BEDROOM must suit the character of the person occupying the room, which means that, in addition to style, personal needs and tastes must also be taken into account. This includes things like the size of the bed, the type of furniture and the lighting. It is also necessary to decide whether or not there is going to be an adjoining bedroom or dressing room.

EL DISEÑO DE CADA DORMITORIO debe ir de acuerdo con la personalidad de quien lo habita, por lo que más allá de buscar estilos hay que atender los gustos y necesidades personales, comenzando por el tamaño de la cama, el tipo de mobiliario, el estilo de ropa de cama, el color de los muros y la clase de iluminación. También hay que decidir si se integran espacios como el baño o el vestidor a la habitación o no.

LE DESIGN D'UNE CHAMBRE A COUCHER doit refléter la personnalité de la personne qui l'utilise. Il ne faut donc pas se contenter de choisir simplement un style en particulier mais prendre en compte les goûts et les nécessités de l'occupant en commençant par la taille du lit, le genre de mobilier, le style de la literie, la couleur des murs et le type d'éclairage. Il faut aussi savoir si l'on décidera de placer dans la chambre une salle de bain ou un dressing.

DAS DESIGN EINES JEDEN SCHLAFZIMMERS sollte mit der Persönlichkeit der Bewohner übereinstimmen. Daher sollten nicht Stilrichtungen, sondern die persönlichen Geschmäcker und Erfordernisse Berücksichtigung finden. Dies beginnt bei der Grösse des Bettes, dem Typ der Möbel, dem Stil der Bettwäsche, der Farbe der Wände und der Art von Beleuchtung. Es ist auch zu entscheiden, ob Bereiche wie Badezimmer und Ankleideraum in das Zimmer integriert werden oder nicht.

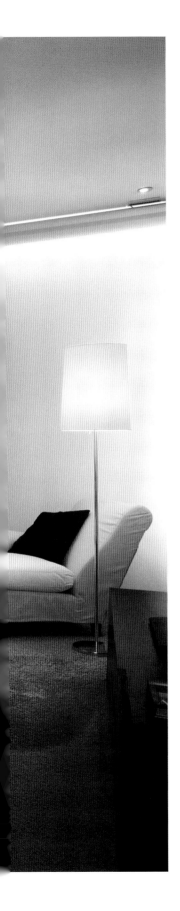

Colored LEDs are wonderful for transforming the tone of a bedroom in a matter of seconds. All it takes is a large white screen, such as curtains, the bed linen, walls and the ceiling, and choosing the desired tone of light at a given moment.

Gracias a los LEDs de colores, hoy en día es posible modificar el aspecto tonal de una habitación en unos segundos. Solamente es necesario crear una pantalla general blanca –cortinas, ropa de cama, muros y techos– y seleccionar el tono de luz que se prefiera al momento.

Grâce aux LEDs de couleurs variées, il est aujourd'hui possible de modifier la teinte de la lumière dans une chambre en quelques secondes. Il est toutefois nécessaire que le blanc domine la pièce (rideaux, literie, murs et plafond) et de bien choisir la teinte de la lumière à un moment déterminé.

Durch die Verwendung von bunten LEDs ist es heute möglich, den farblichen Aspekt eines Raumes in nur Sekunden zu verändern. Es muss nur eine weisse Leinwand geschaffen werden –Vorhänge, Bettwäsche, Wände und Decken– und ein Farbton für das Licht ausgesucht werden, der in diesem Moment bevorzugt wird.

Pure red, orange, burgundy and white combine perfectly in alternation on walls, duvets, headboards, cushions and fittings.

Rojo puro, naranja, vino y blanco son colores que se complementan muy bien al ser utilizados y combinados alternadamente en muros, edredones, cabeceras, cojines y accesorios.

Rouge vif, orange, couleur vin et blanc sont des teintes qui vont très bien ensemble, en particulier lorsqu'elles sont utilisées de manière alternée pour des murs, des couettes, des têtes de lit et certains accessoires.

Pures rot, orange, weinrot und weiss sind Farben, die sich sehr gut ergänzen, wenn sie für Wände, Bettdecken, Kopfenden, Kissen und Accesoires Verwendung finden und abwechselnd kombiniert werden.

Dark wood and white textiles are a must for creating a warm, cozy room. This decorative scheme can be complemented with chocolate-toned leather for the headboard and footboard, which combines readily and looks stylish. A great finishing touch can be provided with red decorative details.

Si se busca un cuarto acogedor y cálido, la madera oscura y los textiles blancos son indispensables. Esta decoración se complementa con piel en tono chocolate para la cabecera y la piesera, un material fácil de combinar y que luce elegante. El toque se puede dar introduciendo detalles en color.

Si l'on souhaite une chambre confortable et chaude, un bois foncé et des tissus blancs sont indispensables. On peut ajouter à ce type de décoration du cuir couleur chocolat pour la tête et la descente de lit car c'est un matériau facile à associer et qui est toujours très esthétique. Et quelques détails de couleur rouge apporteront un plus à la décoration.

Soll ein gemütliches, warmen Zimmer geschaffen werden, sind dunkles Holz und weisse Textilien unabdingbar. Diese Dekoration wird durch Leder in schokoladenbraun am Kopf- und Fussende ergänzt. Es handelt sich dabei um ein Material, das einfach zu kombinieren ist und elegant aussieht. Ein besonderer Touch wird durch den Einbezug von roten Details gegeben.

Kids' bedrooms must take into account the needs and lifestyles of their occupants and be distributed in a functional manner, with sufficient space for playing and/or studying, as well as for resting. Bookshelves are great for maintaining order, but they are equally ideal for storing collections of things like books, records and videos. In many cases, they are part of a study area, attached to a desk. Pure, bright colors are the best bet for these rooms as they are the ones kids usually prefer.

Los dormitorios juveniles deben responder a las necesidades y formas de vida de sus ocupantes y tener una distribución funcional, con espacio suficiente para el ocio y/o el estudio, así como para el descanso. Además de ayudar a mantener un orden, los libreros y repisas son ideales para almacenar colecciones, guardar libros, discos y películas; la mayor parte de ellos integra un área de estudio, desprendiendo un escritorio. Los colores vivos y puros son los más adecuados para estos cuartos, pues son los que generalmente prefieren los jóvenes.

Les chambres d'enfants ou d'adolescents doivent répondre à leurs besoins et être aménagées de façon fonctionnelle avec un espace suffisant pour les loisirs, les études (ou les deux) et le repos. Les bibliothèques intérieures et autres étagères sont idéales non seulement pour qu'il y ait un certain ordre dans la pièce mais aussi pour pouvoir y placer des collections d'objets, des livres, des disques et des films. La plupart des chambres de ce type comprennent un espace propice aux études avec un bureau. Les couleurs vives et pures y sont les plus indiquées car ce sont en général celles que les jeunes préfèrent.

Jugendschlafzimmer müssen die Erfordernisse und Lebensform ihrer Bewohner berücksichtigen und eine praktische Distribution aufweisen, die genügend Platz zum Spielen und/oder Studieren, sowie auch zur Erholung bietet. Regale und Regalbretter helfen dabei, Ordnung zu schaffen und sind ideal zum Aufbewahren von Sammlungen, Büchern, CDs und Filmen. Der grösste Teil bildet eine Art Studio mit einem Schreibtisch. Lebendige, reine Farben sind besonders geeignet für diese Räume, denn sie werden normalerweise von den Jugendlichen bevorzugt.

Rugs are perfect in the bedroom for differentiating between the living areas and the sleeping areas. These spaces can be harmonized if they are made to imitate the style of the bedroom.

Los tapetes son perfectos en las recámaras para precisar cuáles son las áreas de estar y cuáles las de dormir. Para unificar se aconseja que empaten con el estilo de la recámara.

Les tapis sont parfaits dans une chambre pour séparer les espaces détentes de l'endroit où l'on dort. Pour cependant harmoniser l'ensemble, il est conseillé d'utiliser des tapis dont le style reflète celui de la chambre.

Teppiche sind in Schlafzimmern dazu geeignet, den Aufenthaltsbereich vom Schlafbereich abzugrenzen. Um die Einheitlichkeit zu gewährliesten, sollte die Stilrichtung des Schlafzimmer eingehalten werden.

These rooms are intended for rest, but they are also places of leisure and/or personal development. As a result, at the risk of seeming repetitive, placing a chaise long at the foot of the bed offers a good way to fulfill these last two activities.

Además de para reposar, las habitaciones se conceptualizan también como espacios para el ocio y/o para el desarrollo personal. Por lo que, aún a riesgo de parecer repetitivos, colocar un buen chaise long a los pies de la cama, puede servir para desempeñar adecuadamente estas dos últimas actividades.

Les chambres sont des espaces pour se reposer mais aussi des lieux conçus pour les loisirs ou pour mieux se retrouver avec soi-même. Aussi est-il recommandé, même si cela peut paraître superfétatoire, d'y placer une chaise longue aux pieds du lit pour pouvoir confortablement se livrer à ces activités.

Ausser zum Ruhen sind Schlafzimmer auch für die Freizeitgestaltung und/oder die persönliche Entwicklung geeignet. In diesem Zusammenhang ist erneut zu wiederholen, dass ein schönes Sofa am Fusse des Bettes dazu geeignet ist, diese beiden letzteren Aktivitäten durchzuführen.

An attractive and all-encompassing ambience is created by using chocolate brown wood on the walls, floors and bureaus, especially if a contrast is generated between the whites of the bed linen and soffit and the rawer tones of the upholstery.

Generar un entorno envolvente colocando madera color chocolate en pisos, muros y buroes puede resultar muy atractivo, si se provoca que actúe por contraste con la ropa de cama y el plafón en blanco puro y la tapicería de una sala en crudo.

Entourer la pièce avec du bois de couleur chocolat pour les sols, les murs et les tables de nuit peut se révéler très esthétique si on joue sur le contraste créé avec la literie et le faux-plafond de couleur blanche et les tapis d'un salon de couleur écrue.

Die Verwendung von dunkelbraunem Holz für Böden, Wände und Nachttische kann sehr attraktiv sein, sofern diese mit der Bettwäsche und der Decke in purem weiss, sowie dem naturweissen Stoff der Sitzgelegenheit kontrastieren.

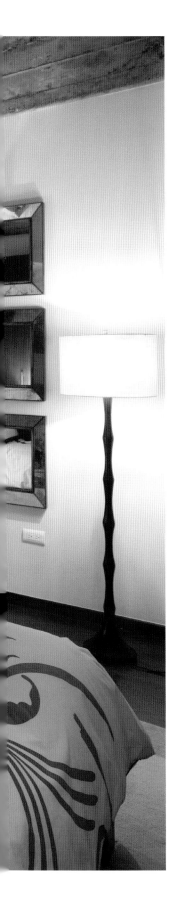

The pure and simple lines of modern-day bedroom furniture and the formal purity of its design vitalize the space and turn the bed into a valuable component. In this type of arrangement, duvets and cushions take on a leading role.

El trazo puro y sencillo del mobiliario contemporáneo para recámara y la pureza formal de su diseño le imprimen fuerza al espacio y convierten a la cama en un mueble posible de ser valorizado. En estos ambientes edredones y cojines se convierten en protagonistas.

Le tracé simple et pur du mobilier moderne pour des chambres à coucher et la pureté formelle de son design donnent de la force à l'espace et transforment le lit en meuble protagoniste de la décoration. Avec ce genre d'atmosphère, la couette et les oreillers jouent également un rôle essentiel.

Die klaren und einfachen Linien der modernen Möbel für Schlafzimmer und die formelle Reinheit des Designs verleihen dem Raum Stärke und werten das Bett als Möbel auf. In diesen Atmosphären werden Bettdecken und Kissen zu den Hauptdarstellern.

If the size of the space allows it, the bedroom can be incorporated into a lounge, a study or a TV room, making sure suitable distances are kept between the different areas and that there are no obstructions to free movement between them.

Si las dimensiones lo permiten es factible integrar a la habitación una sala, un estudio y un área de TV, procurando sanas distancias entre uno y otro, y cuidando no obstaculizar las circulaciones.

Lorsque les dimensions le permettent, il est possible de prévoir un salon, un bureau et un coin télé dans une chambre si l'on préserve une certaine distance entre les espaces et si les zones de passages restent dégagées.

Wenn die Ausmasse dies zulassen, kann im Raum eine Sitzecke, ein Studio oder ein Fernsehbereich eingeplant werden. Dabei sollte ein gesunder Abstand zwischen den Bereichen eingehalten und der Durchgang nicht behindert werden.

In terms of function, cushions can make a major contribution to the decoration of the bedroom, but they can also enrich it with shapes, textures, patterns and colors.

Desde el punto de vista funcional, los cojines son elementos decorativos de suma importancia en los dormitorios, pero también sirven para añadir formas, texturas, dibujos y colores en una habitación.

D'un point de vue fonctionnel, les oreillers et autres coussins sont des éléments décoratifs très importants dans les chambres à coucher car ils apportent formes, textures, motifs et couleurs supplémentaires à la pièce.

Vom funktionellen Gesichtspunkt aus sind Kissen höchst wichtige Dekorationselemente in Schlafzimmern, die auch dazu dienen, einen Raum mit Formen, Texturen, Mustern und Farben zu versehen.

architectonic arquitectónicos architectoniques architektonische

solórzano, *architectural project:* sergio barrera, *contributor:* luis alfonso g., (bottom right) *architectural project:* PASCAL ARQUITECTOS, carlos pascal wolf y gerard pascal wolf

61 (top left) *architectural project:* DESIGN PRIMARIO, guillermo quintanilla, (top right) *interior design project:* KA INTERNACIONAL, margarita solórzano, *architectural project:* sergio barrera, *contributor:* luis alfonso g., (bottom) *interior design project:* MARQCÓ, mariangel álvarez c. y covadonga hernández g., *contributor:* maira santos

62-63 *architectural project:* DM ARQUITECTOS, javier duarte morales

65 *architectural project:* RDLP ARQUITECTOS, *architectural supervision:* rodrigo de la peña l. y víctor montalvo, *design team:* jessica patrón y esther rosales

66-67 *architectural project:* NOGAL ARQUITECTOS, josé m. nogal moragues

68-69 *architectural project:* DM ARQUITECTOS, javier duarte morales

70 (left) *architectural project and interior design:* ARQUITECTURA E INTERIORES, andrea vincze, *contributor:* héctor esrawe, (right) *interior design project:* COVILHA, blanca gonzález, maribel gonzález y mely gonzález, *architectural project:* javier sordo madaleno

71 (left) *architectural project:* MARTINEZ&SORDO, carlos garcía jaime, *interior design project:* MARTINEZ&SORDO, juan salvador martínez y luis martín sordo, *contributors:* adela rodríguez y pilar peñalver clemente, (right) *architectural project:* GRUPO LBC, alfonso lópez baz, javier calleja y eduardo hernández, *furniture design and selection:* carlos majluf y simón hamui

72-73 *architectural project:* GLR ARQUITECTOS, gilberto l. rodríguez, *contributors:* enrique salas, cecilia bautista, oscar o'farrill

74 *interior design project:* ADI, gina parlange pizarro

75 *architectural project:* GA, GRUPO ARQUITECTURA, daniel álvarez

76 *architectural project:* CASAS DE MÉXICO Y DESARROLLOS

77 *architectural project:* OF-A, jihei aoki, alejandro cortés, constanze martens y carlos gonzález

78-79 *architectural project:* ART ARQUITECTOS, antonio rueda ventosa

80 *architectural project:* PASCAL ARQUITECTOS, carlos pascal wolf y gerard pascal wolf

81 (top) *architectural project:* PASCAL ARQUITECTOS, carlos pascal wolf y gerard pascal wolf, (bottom) *interior design project:* MARQCÓ, mariangel álvarez c. y covadonga hernández g., *architectural project:* TARME, alex carranza y gerardo ruiz, *contributor:* maira santos

82 *interior design project:* EZEQUIELFARCA, ezequiel farca, *contributors:* luis alberto romero y valencia, valeria tamayo, mónica garcía y paulina sarquís

83 *interior design project:* EZEQUIELFARCA, ezequiel farca, *contributors:* erika ibarra, isela rivera y mónica garcía

84 *architectural project:* GUZMÁN Y OGARRIO ARQUITECTOS, jaime guzmán g. y fernando ogarrio k.

85 *architectural project:* ABAX, fernando de haro, jesús fernández, omar fuentes y bertha figueroa

86-87 *architectural project:* RDLP ARQUITECTOS y antonio ramírez, *architectural supervision:* rodrigo de la peña l. y víctor montalvo, *design team:* aranzazú fernández

88 *architectural project:* DPGa, daniel pérez gil

89 (top) *architectural project:* FCA, francisco e. carbajal, *contributor:* gabriela sánchez, (bottom) *architectural project:* DPGa, daniel pérez gil

90 *architectural project:* GGAD, gerardo garcía lópez

91 (top) *architectural project:* RDLP ARQUITECTOS, *architectural supervision:* rodrigo de la peña l. y víctor montalvo, *design team:* adolfo elizondo, (bottom) *architectural project:* INTERARQ, david penjos

92 (left) *architectural project:* AGRAZ ARQUITECTOS, ricardo agraz, *contributors:* jessica magaña, alberto tacher, sara tamez, (top) *architectural project:* C'CÚBICA, emilio cabrero, andrea cesarman y marco a. coello buck, (bottom) *architectural project:* ABAX, fernando de haro, jesús fernández, omar fuentes y bertha figueroa

93 (top) *architectural and interior design project:* GGAD, gerardo garcía lópez, (bottom) *architectural project:* GARDUÑO ARQUITECTOS, juan garduño, ernesto flores, ricardo guzmán, daniel banda, isaac romero, athos sajid, *construction:* ALEN CONSTRUCCIONES, enrique álvarez.

94-95 *architectural project:* VELA ARQUITECTOS, ernesto vela ruiz

96 *interior design project:* COVILHA, blanca gonzález, maribel gonzález y mely gonzález

97 *architectural project:* DM ARQUITECTOS, javier duarte morales

98-99 *architectural project:* HASBANI ARQUITECTOS, mayer hasbani, *contributors:* omar salas

100 *architectural project:* MYG ARQUITECTOS, adriana garcía o.

101 *interior design project:* ADI, gina parlange pizarro, *architectural project:* ABAX, fernando de haro, jesús fernández, omar fuentes y bertha figueroa, *contributors:* anna grendys, mónica maza y pía cozzi

102 (left) *interior design project:* MARQCÓ, mariangel álvarez c. y covadonga hernández g., *architectural project:* TARME, alex carranza y gerardo ruiz, *contributor:* mónica saucedo, (top) *architectural project:* GRUPO LBC, alfonso lópez baz, javier calleja y eduardo hernández, *furniture design and selection:* carlos majluf y simón hamui, (bottom) *architectural project:* GUZMÁN Y OGARRIO ARQUITECTOS, jaime guzmán g. y fernando ogarrio k.

104-105 *architectural project:* JSª, javier sánchez, juan manuel soler, tristán ossola, diana elizalde

106 *architectural project:* TARME, alex carranza y gerardo ruiz díaz

107 *interior design project:* ADI, gina parlange pizarro, *architectural project:* ABAX, fernando de haro, jesús fernández, omar fuentes y bertha figueroa, *contributors:* anna grendys, mónica maza y pía cozzi

108 *architectural project:* JUAN CARLOS AVILES ARQUITECTOS, juan carlos aviles iguiniz

109 *architectural project:* GRUPO LBC, alfonso lópez baz, javier calleja y eduardo hernández, *furniture design and selection:* carlos majluf y simón hamui

110-111 *architectural project:* DM ARQUITECTOS, javier duarte morales

112-113 *architectural project:* GRUPO LBC, alfonso lópez baz, javier calleja y eduardo hernández, *furniture design and selection:* carlos majluf y simón hamui

114-115 *interior design project:* DUPUIS, alejandra prieto y cecilia prieto, *architectural project:* JSª, javier sánchez

116-117 *interior design project:* ARQUITECTURA DE INTERIORES, marisabel gómez vázquez, *design team:* marisol tafich santos, josé luis orozco soto

118-119 *architectural project:* ANONIMOUS-LED, alfonso jiménez, marco a. velázquez y jorge plascencia

120-121 *architectural project:* MYG ARQUITECTOS, adriana garcía o.

122 *architectural and construction project:* HASBANI ARQUITECTOS, mayer hasbani, *contributors:* omar salas, *instalation:* instalaciones 2000

123 *architectural project:* VELA ARQUITECTOS, ernesto vela ruiz

124 *architectural project:* JSª DISEÑO Y DESARROLLO, javier sánchez, lorenia castillo, roberto lascano, y rubén lechuga

125 *architectural project:* federico gómez crespo

126-127 *architectural project:* JHG, jorge hernández de la garza

128-129 *architectural project:* DM ARQUITECTOS, javier duarte morales

130 *architectural project:* GRUPO LBC, alfonso lópez baz y javier calleja, *furniture design and selection:* carlos majluf y simón hamui

131 *architectural project:* GRUPO LBC, alfonso lópez baz y javier calleja

132-133 architectural project: OF-A, jihei aoki, alejandro cortés, constanze martens y carlos gonzález

134-135 *architectural project:* GA, GRUPO ARQUITECTURA, daniel álvarez

136 *interior design project:* EZEQUIELFARCA, ezequiel farca, *contributors:* luis alberto romero y valencia, valeria tamayo, mónica garcía y paulina sarquís

137 (top) *interior design project:* DECORÉ INTERIORISMO, maría patricia díaz de león, maría elena díaz de león

137 (bottom) *interior design project:* EZEQUIELFARCA, ezequiel farca, *contributors:* luis alberto romero y valencia, valeria tamayo, mónica garcía y paulina sarquís

138 *architectural project:* C'CÚBICA, emilio cabrero, andrea cesarman y marco a. coello buck

139 (center and right) *architectural project:* PASCAL ARQUITECTOS, carlos pascal wolf y gerard pascal wolf

140-141 *architectural project:* ARTECK / TORBELI, francisco guzmán-giraud y elena talavera

142 (top left and right) *interior design project:* TERRÉS, javier valenzuela g., fernando valenzuela g. y guillermo valenzuela g. (bottom) MARQCÓ, mariangel álvarez c. y covadonga hernández g., *contributor:* maira santos

143 (top) *architectural project:* TARME, alex carranza valles y gerardo ruiz díaz, (bottom) *interior design:* MARQCÓ, mariangel álvarez c. y covadonga hernández g., *contributor:* maira santos

144 *architectural project:* GA, GRUPO ARQUITECTURA, daniel álvarez

145 *architectural project:* DM ARQUITECTOS, javier duarte morales

146-147 *architectural and interior design project:* ARQUITECTURA E INTERIORES, andrea vincze

148 *interior design project:* C-CHIC, olga mussali h. y sara mizrahi e.

149 *architectural project:* EXTRACTO, robert duarte y vanessa patiño, *contributors:* amaury peña g., jonathan aguayo, daniel reyes l., mario dorantes, raquel maricruz garcía, alejandra martínez l., javier rivero d. y manuel quiroz o.

150-151 *architectural project:* ANONIMOUS-LED, alfonso jiménez, marco a. velázquez y jorge plascencia

152 *architectural project:* ABAX, fernando de haro, jesús fernández, omar fuentes y bertha figueroa

152 (bottom) *architectural project:* ALCOCER ARQUITECTOS, guillermo alcocer

153 (bottom)ABAX, fernando de haro, jesús fernández, omar fuentes y bertha figueroa

154 *architectural project:* NOGAL ARQUITECTOS, josé m. nogal moragues

156-157 *architectural project:* ANONIMOUS-LED, alfonso jiménez, marco a. velázquez y jorge plascencia

158 *architectural project:* JUAN CARLOS AVILES ARQUITECTOS, juan carlos aviles iguiniz

159 *architectural project:* FM ARQUITECTURA, felipe martínez tirado

160-161 *architectural project:* GA, GRUPO ARQUITECTURA, daniel álvarez

162 *architectural and interior design project:* JOSÉ ANTONIO MADRID ARQUITECTOS, josé antonio madrid

163 *architectural project:* VELA ARQUITECTOS, ernesto vela ruiz

164-165 *architectural project:* C'CÚBICA, emilio cabrero, andrea cesarman y marco a. coello buck

166 (top) *architectural and art consultancy project:* EXTRACTO, robert duarte y vanessa patiño, *contributors:* jorge rodríguez y juan carlos domínguez, *construction:* jorge rodríguez

166 (bottom) *architectural project:* GLR ARQUITECTOS, gilberto l. rodríguez

167 *interior design project:* DIARQ, gina diez barroso de franklin

168-169 *architectural project:* JHG, jorge hernández de la garza

170, 171 (top) *architectural project:* DPGa, daniel pérez-gil, *contributor:* sergio reinoso y juan a. fragoso

171 (bottom) *architectural project:* EXTRACTO, robert duarte y vanessa patiño, *contributors:* amaury peña g., daniel reyes l., raquel maricruz garcía, alejandra martínez l., javier rivero d., manuel quiroz o. y mario dorantes

172 *architectural project:* HASBANI ARQUITECTOS, mayer hasbani, *contributor:* omar salas

173 *interior design project:* EZEQUIELFARCA, ezequiel farca, *contributors:* erika ibarra, isela rivera y mónica garcía

174 (top)-175 *architectural project:* RDLP ARQUITECTOS, rodrigo de la peña l., *design team:* georgina pérez, *architectural supervision:* rodrigo de la peña y víctor montalvo, *structural engineering:* fernando montemayor

174 (bottom) *architectural project:* GRUPO ARQEE, pedro escobar f v., jorge escalante p. y jorge carral d.

176 (top left and bottom) *architectural project:* GRUPO CORAGGIO, rubén basurto gómez, (top right) *interior design project:* DESIGN PRIMARIO, josé guillermo quintana cancino

177 (top) *architectural project:* RDLP ARQUITECTOS, rodrigo de la peña l., *design team:* aranzazú fernández, *architectural supervision:* rodrigo de la peña y víctor montalvo, (bottom) *architectural project:* A-001 TALLER DE ARQUITECTURA, eduardo gorozpe fernández

178 *architectural project:* INTERDESIGNOK, oscar gutiérrez moreno

179 *architectural project:* ANONIMOUS-LED, alfonso jiménez, marco a. velázquez y jorge plascencia

180-181 *architectural project:* EXTRACTO, robert duarte y vanessa patiño, *contributors:* amaury peña g., jonathan aguayo, daniel reyes l., mario dorantes, raquel maricruz garcía, alejandra martínez l., javier rivero d. y manuel quiroz o.

182 (left) *architectural project:* ANONIMOUS-LED, alfonso jiménez, marco a. velázquez y jorge plascencia, (right) *architectural project:* ABAX, fernando de haro, jesús fernández, omar fuentes y bertha figueroa

183 *architectural project:* ABAX, fernando de haro, jesús fernández, omar fuentes y bertha figueroa

185 *interior design project:* GARDUÑO ARQUITECTOS, juan garduño, ernesto flores, ricardo guzmán, daniel banda, isaac romero y athos sajid, *construction:* ALEN CONSTRUCCIONES, enrique álvarez

186 (top left and bottom) *architectural project:* JHG, jorge hernández de la garza, (top right) *interior design project:* GARDUÑO ARQUITECTOS, juan garduño, ernesto flores, ricardo guzmán, daniel banda, isaac romero y athos sajid, *construction:* ALEN CONSTRUCCIONES, enrique álvarez

187 *architectural project:* JHG, jorge hernández de la garza

188-189 y 190 *architectural project:* GA, GRUPO ARQUITECTURA, daniel álvarez

191-192 *interior design project:* GARDUÑO ARQUITECTOS, juan garduño, ernesto flores, ricardo guzmán, daniel banda, isaac romero y athos sajid, *construction:* ALEN CONSTRUCCIONES, enrique álvarez

193 *architectural project:* EXTRACTO, robert duarte y vanessa patiño, *contributors:* amaury peña g., jonathan aguayo, daniel reyes l., mario dorantes, raquel maricruz garcía, alejandra martínez l., javier rivero d. y manuel quiroz o.

194 *architectural project:* PASCAL ARQUITECTOS, carlos pascal wolf y gerard pascal wolf

195 *interior design project:* EZEQUIELFARCA, ezequiel farca, *contributors:* erika ibarra, isela rivera y mónica garcía

197 (top) *architectural project:* RDLP ARQUITECTOS, rodrigo de la peña l., *design team:* aranzazú fernández, *architectural supervision:* rodrigo de la peña y víctor montalvo, (bottom) *architectural project:* GUTIÉRREZ-ALONSO ARQUITECTURA/ SILVIA DECANINI ARQUITECTOS eduardo gutiérrez guzmán, ángel alonso chein y silvia decanini terán, *contributors:* sergio valdés, venus zepeda, b&b iuminación, gerson huerta y martha gaos

198 *interior design project:* EZEQUIELFARCA, ezequiel farca, *contributors:* luis alberto romero y valencia, valeria tamayo, mónica garcía y paulina sarquís

199 *interior design project:* EZEQUIELFARCA, ezequiel farca, *contributors:* erika ibarra, isela rivera y mónica garcía

200-201 *architectural project:* RDLP ARQUITECTOS, rodrigo de la peña l., *design team:* georgina pérez, *architectural supervision:* rodrigo de la peña y víctor montalvo

202-203 *interior design:* KARAT, karla atristain r., *architectural project:* MOBILARQ horacio pinto r., *contributors:* luis antonio luna y dalia arreola

204-205 (top and center) *architectural project:* ABAX, fernando de haro, jesús fernández, omar fuentes y bertha figueroa

205 (bottom), 206 (left) *interior design project:* EZEQUIELFARCA, ezequiel farca, *contributors:* erika ibarra, isela rivera y mónica garcía, (right) *architectural project:* GRUPO LBC, alfonso lópez baz, javier calleja y eduardo hernández, *furniture design and selection:* carlos majluf y simón hamui

207 *architectural and interior design project:* GGAD, gerardo garcía lópez

208 *interior design project:* GARDUÑO ARQUITECTOS, juan garduño, ernesto flores, ricardo guzmán, daniel banda, isaac romero y athos sajid, *construction:* ALEN CONSTRUCCIONES, enrique álvarez

209 *architectural project:* OF-A, jihei aoki, alejandro cortés, constanze martens y carlos gonzález

210-211 *interior design project:* GARDUÑO ARQUITECTOS, juan garduño, ernesto flores, ricardo guzmán, daniel banda, isaac romero y athos sajid, *construction:* ALEN CONSTRUCCIONES, enrique álvarez

213 (top) *architectural and interior design project:* ART ARQUITECTOS, antonio rueda ventosa, (bottom) *architectural and interior design project:* GRUPO DIARQ CALIFORNIA, gina diez barroso de franklin

214 *architectural project:* EXTRACTO, robert duarte y vanessa patiño, *contributors:* amaury peña g., jonathan aguayo, daniel reyes l., mario dorantes, raquel maricruz garcía, alejandra martínez l., javier rivero d., manuel quiroz o.

215 *interior design project:* GRUPO DIARQ CALIFORNIA, gina diez barroso de franklin

216 (top left) *architectural project:* MYG ARQUITECTOS, adriana garcía o., (top center, center left) *architectural project:* AGRAZ ARQUITECTOS, ricardo agraz. (top right) *interior design project:* GRUPO AGM, patricio garcía muriel y fernando abogado alonso, (center) *architectural project:* C'CÚBICA, emilio cabrero, andrea cesarman y marco a. coello buck, (center right) *architectural project:* DI VECE Y ASOCIADOS ARQUITECTOS, paolino di vece roux, *contributors:* cony lupercio, luis enrique reynoso, *interior design project:* laura orozco, (bottom left) *interior design project:* GRUPO DIARQ CALIFORNIA, gina diez barroso de franklin, (bottom center) *architectural project:* DPGa, daniel pérez-gil, *contributors:* sergio reinoso y juan a. fragoso, (bottom right) *architectural project:* GLR ARQUITECTOS, gilberto l. rodríguez

217 *architectural project:* GUTIÉRREZ Y ALONSO ARQUITECTOS, ángel alonso chein y eduardo gutiérrez guzmán, *contributors:* luis segura, rodrigo turati, vicente laso, gabriela vázquez del mercado, gerson huerta y A PLENO SOL

218 *architectural project:* ABAX, fernando de haro, jesús fernández, omar fuentes y bertha figueroa, *interior design project:* MARQCÓ, mariangel álvarez c. y covadonga hernández g.

219 GRUPO LBC alfonso lópez baz, javier calleja y eduardo hernández, *furniture design and selection:* carlos majluf y simón hamui

220 (top) *interior design project:* EZEQUIELFARCA, ezequiel farca, *contributors:* erika ibarra, isela rivera y mónica garcía, (bottom) *architectural project:* JUAN CARLOS AVILÉS ARQUITECTOS, juan carlos avilés iguiniz

221 (top) *architectural project:* ABAX, fernando de haro, jesús fernández, omar fuentes y bertha figueroa, (bottom) *interior design project:* ARMELLA ARQUITECTOS, mario armella maza y mario armella gullette, *contributors:* jorge rodríguez l. y alejandra valdivia

222-223 *architectural project:* EXTRACTO, robert duarte y vanessa patiño, *contributors:* jorge rodríguez y juan carlos domínguez

224-225 *interior design project:* EZEQUIELFARCA, ezequiel farca, *contributors:* erika ibarra, isela rivera y mónica garcía,

227 *architectural project:* HASBANI ARQUITECTOS, mayer hasbani, *contributors:* omar salas, *instalation:* instalaciones 2000

228 *interior design project:* MODA IN CASA, louis poiré, *architectural project:* miguel ángel aragonés

229 *architectural project:* EXTRACTO, robert duarte y vanessa patiño, *contributors:* jorge rodríguez y juan carlos domínguez

231 *interior design project:* KA INTERNACIONAL, margarita solórzano

232 *interior design project:* TERRÉS, javier valenzuela g., fernando valenzuela g. y guillermo valenzuela g.

233 *interior design project:* MARQCÓ, mariangel álvarez y covadonga hernández

234-235 *furniture design:* TORBELI, elena talavera, *architectural project:* ARTECK, francisco guzmán-giraud

236 *interior design project:* KARAT, karla atristain r., *architectural project:* MOBILARQ, horacio pinto r., *contributors:* luis antonio luna y dalia arreola

237 (top) *interior design project:* ECLÉCTICA DISEÑO, mónica hernández sadurni, *architectural project:* fernando montes de oca pineda, *project implementation:* juan cabrera aceves, (bottom) *interior design project:* EZEQUIELFARCA, ezequiel farca, *contributors:* luis alberto romero y valencia, valeria tamayo, mónica garcía y paulina sarquís

238-239 *interior design project:* EZEQUIELFARCA, ezequiel farca, *contributors:* erika ibarra, isela rivera y mónica garcía

240 (top left) *interior design project:* C CHIC, olga mussali h. y sara mizrahi e. (top right and bottom) *interior design project:* KARAT, karla atristain rodríguez, *architectural project:* MOBILARQ, horacio pinto rodríguez, *contributors:* luis antonio luna y dalia arreola

241 *interior design project:* C-CHIC, olga mussali h. y sara mizrahi e.

242-243 *architectural and interior project:* JSª DISEÑO Y DESARROLLO, javier sánchez, paola calzada, larissa kadner, alejandro zárate y cecilia solís

244 *interior design project:* EZEQUIELFARCA, ezequiel farca, *contributors:* luis alberto romero y valencia, valeria tamayo, mónica garcía y paulina sarquís

245 *interior design project:* EZEQUIELFARCA, ezequiel farca, *contributors:* erika ibarra, isela rivera y mónica garcía,

246-247 *architectural project:* GA, GRUPO ARQUITECTURA, daniel álvarez

248 architectural project: OF-A, jihei aoki, alejandro cortés, constanze martens y carlos gonzález

249 *architectural project:* EXTRACTO, robert duarte y vanessa patiño, *contributors:* amaury peña g., jonathan aguayo, daniel reyes l., mario dorantes, raquel maricruz garcía, alejandra martínez l., javier rivero d., manuel quiroz o.,

250 *architectural project:* GLR ARQUITECTOS, gilberto l. rodríguez, *contributors:* bernardo chapa, joaquín jenis, tomás güereña, diana guerra, eduardo fuentes

251 *architectural and interior design project:* ART ARQUITECTOS, antonio rueda ventosa

252 *interior design project:* MARQCÓ, mariangel álvarez c. y covadonga hernández g., *architectural project:* TARME, alex carranza y gerardo ruiz

253 *interior design project:* C'CÚBICA, emilio cabrero, andrea cesarman y marco a. coello buck
254-255 *interior design project:* ECLÉCTICA DISEÑO, mónica hernández sadurni
257 (top) *interior design project:* ADI, gina parlange pizarro, (bottom) *architectural project:* ABAX, fernando de haro, jesús fernández, omar fuentes y bertha figueroa

photographic fotográficos photographiques fotografische

alberto moreno - pgs.197 (bottom), 217, 221 (bottom).

alejandra catala - pgs. 167, 215, 216 (bottom left).

alejandra vega - pgs. 45 ,216 (top right).

alfonso de béjar - pgs. 84, 102 (bottom), 125, 152 (bottom), 204-205 (top and center), 218, 221 (top), 228.

angelo de stefani h. - pgs. 237 (top), 254-255.

arturo chávez - pgs. 114-115.

carlos díaz corona - pg. 44.

carlos medina vega - pgs. 60 (bottom left), 61 (top right) 231.

cathie ferguson - pgs. 92 (bottom), 183, 257 (bottom).

eduardo dayan - pg. 213 (bottom).

eric lira: pg. 148

fabiola menchelli - pgs. 52-53 (center), 54 (left), 60 (top right),142 (top), 232.

francisco e. carbajal - pg. 89 (top).

francisco lubbert - pgs. 10 (right), 26-27, 100, 120-121, 216 (top left)

héctor armando herrera - pgs. 88, 89 (bottom), 170 -171 (top).

héctor velasco facio - pgs. 3, 9, 10 (left),11 (right), 28-29, 48, 54 (bottom), 55, 58-59, 61 (bottom), 62-63, 68-69, 70 (right), 71, 77, 81, 85, 93 (top), 96, 97, 98-99, 102 (top left), 106, 108 a 113, 122, 124, 128 a 133, 140, 142 (bottom), 143, 145, 158, 162, 172, 206 (right), 207, 209, 219, 227, 233 a 235, 248, 252.

jair navarrete - pgs. 104-105.

jaime navarro - pgs. 20-21 (left), 70, 74, 80-81 (top),101, 107, 146-147, 242-243, 257 (top)

joaquín cabeza - pg. 49.

jordi farré - pg. 90.

jorge rodríguez almanza - pgs. 24-25, 166 (top), 222-223, 229.

jorge silva - pgs. 60 (top left), 76, 92 (top), 138 (left), 164, 216 (center), 253.

jorge taboada - pgs. 36-37, 50-51, 54 (top right), 65, 72-73, 86-87, 91 (top), 94-95, 123, 159, 163,166 (bottom),174 (top), 175, 177 (top), 197 (top), 200-201, 216 (bottom right), 250.

juan josé diaz infante - pg. 141.

laura cohen - pgs. 19 (bottom), 38-39, 93 (bottom), 185, 186 (top right), 191, 192, 208, 210-211.

lumbrera - pgs. 53 (top and bottom), 137 (top).

leonardo walter - pgs. 46-47, 149, 171 (bottom), 180-181, 193, 214, 249.

luz maría sánchez - pgs. 61 (top left), 176 (top right).

maayan jinich - pg. 241 (top).

manuel garcía y ma.isabel santaularia - pg. 177 (bottom).

marisol paredes - pgs. 78-79, 213 (top), 251.

mark callanan - pgs. 152-153 (top and bottom), 182 (right)

mauricio avramow - pg. 165

michael calderwood - pg. 178.

mito covarrubias - pgs. 22-23, 92 (left), 216 (top center, center left, center right).

paul czitrom - pgs. 4-5, 14-15, 32-33, 40-41, 75, 82-83, 126-127, 134 a 136, 137 (bottom), 144, 160-161, 168-169, 173, 186 (top left and bottom), 18/ to 190, 195, 198-199, 205 (bottom), 206 (left), 220 (top), 224-225, 237 (bottom), 238-239, 244 a 247.

ricardo janet - pgs. 11 (left), 16, 18-19 (top), 118-119, 150-151, 156-157, 179, 182 (left).

rigoberto moreno - pgs. 116-117.

sófocles hernández - pgs. 8, 42-43, 60 (bottom right), 194, 139 (center and right).

uriel sasson - pg. 240 (top left).

verónica garcía - pgs. 56-5/ 202-203, 236, 240 (top rigth and bottom)

víctor benítez - pgs. 31, 66-67, 154,

víctor tovar hernández - pgs. 34-35, 91 (bottom).

Se terminó de imprimir el mes de Enero del 2010 en China. El cuidado de la edición estuvo a cargo de AM Editores S.A. de C.V. Printed in January 2010 in China. Published by AM Editores S.A. de C.V.